Praise for *The Financial Aid Handbook*

"The first two chapters alone are worth the price of admission! *The Financial Aid Handbook* offers students—and their families— a lot of wise and practical advice on making the cost of college to be more affordable and more acceptable. A topic like student loan indebtedness is never an easy subject for a family to discuss at the 'kitchen table of life.' Carol Stack and Ruth Vedvik have produced a comprehensive review of the financial aid process, with the purposeful intent of helping students to make wise choices. Their message is spot on! Honestly, you cannot afford to not take their advice!"

—Phil Trout, College Counselor, Minnetonka High School, past president, National Association of College Admission Counselors (NACAC)

"I use *The Financial Aid Handbook* to train admission counselors and financial aid staff new to the profession on the basics of financial aid. My favorite chapters are 'myths,' 'basics,' 'parents,' and 'everything you need to know.' After 24 years in the profession, I sometimes forget the need to initially coach young enrollment management professionals without using terms that are too technical. While FSA Coach is the expert technical coach, *The Financial Aid Handbook* is written in a manner that makes the information more digestible—it can be read over a weekend. Plus, the Handbook is helpful in coaching staff on how to communicate with families and make financial aid less daunting. A stack of edition two—and previously edition one—sits on my bookshelf to give to every new hire on my team."

—Kim Johnson, vice president for Enrollment Management, Vanguard University

"As a parent of a college-bound teenager, I found this was the right book at the right time for me. Each chapter felt like a one-on-one financial aid session with the authors. They've literally written the book on how to find the best-fit, best-value college. I can't imagine trying to navigate the world of college financial aid without the help of this book. Whenever friends my age talk about untangling the financial aid process, I tell them to stop guessing the secrets and simply read this book."

—Colin Sokolowski, education communication professional
and high school parent

THE
FINANCIAL AID HANDBOOK

REVISED EDITION

Getting the Education You Want for the Price You Can Afford

CAROL STACK and RUTH VEDVIK

CAREER
PRESS

THE FINANCIAL AID HANDBOOK, REVISED EDITION
TYPESET BY PERFECTYPE, NASHVILLE, TENN.
Original cover design by Rob Johnson/toprotype
Mortar board image by alexsl/istock
Printed in the U.S.A.

To order this title, please call toll-free 1-800-CAREER-1 (NJ and Canada: 201-848-0310) to order using VISA or MasterCard, or for further information on books from Career Press.

The Career Press, Inc.
12 Parish Drive
Wayne, NJ 07470
www.careerpress.com

Library of Congress Cataloging-in-Publication Data

CIP Data Available Upon Request.

ACKNOWLEDGMENTS

SPECIAL THANKS TO Barbara, our secret weapon!

Lots of love to David, Craig, Krista, and Ian for their patience and support, and Krista for her contribution.

We'd like to extend an enormous thank-you to our agent Joelle Delbourgo. And to the staff at Career Press for encouraging us to do a Revised Edition.

We'd also like to thank our colleagues who aided us enormously—either by reading, critiquing, or just plain listening. You are all brilliant, helpful, and kind. Thank you for your help, your conversation, and your friendship.

This book couldn't exist without all of the students, parents, and guidance counselors we have had the privilege of serving throughout the years.

CONTENTS

PREFACE FOR THE REVISED EDITION

WHEN WE WROTE *The Financial Aid Handbook* in 2011, our primary focus was to help students and parents gain control over the extraordinary cost of a college education.

Since then we have had hundreds of wonderful conversations over email, phone, at conferences, on planes, trains, and at PTA meetings with families who have read, enjoyed, and benefitted from this book, and we've learned a few new things about what you're looking for. Many things have changed in the past five years: the web has become more robust, and there are new (and terrific) websites out there with brand new sets of data and information. The federal government has made some changes to the FAFSA, and now it is both easier to complete and available to students earlier in the process. The testing companies have changed, too; there is a new SAT as of March 2016, and ACT has dropped the ACT PLAN. We have used "old" SAT scores in this edition, knowing that many students will have both old and new, but they can easily be converted to one another at the collegereadiness.collegeboard .org website.

In this new edition we updated almost all of our numbers, but the central focus of the book remains the same: to help you understand the process and guide you through the cost-conscious search.

We look forward to hearing feedback about this new edition from a new generation of students and parents, on planes, on trains, in school auditoriums, boardrooms, and over email anytime.

Yours,
Carol Stack and Ruth Vedvik

INTRODUCTION FOR PARENTS

THE TIME IS finally here to send your baby off to college. We recommend kick-starting the process with two books: ours (more on that in a minute) and *Letting Go: A Parent's Guide to Understanding the College Years* by Karen Levin Coburn and Madge Lawrence Treeger (a fabulous and insightful description of what it really means when your child goes off to college).

You can't help but notice that we've addressed this book to students—our reasoning for that is simple. Even though we know that the decision to select a particular college or university is usually a family decision—the process itself—ranging from the first request for information to the application, essay, letters of reference, and many of the financial aid forms—is for the student to complete. It is vital that students take ownership of the process with the best information possible. Like you, we know the difficulty of engaging the attention of a high school student in a confusing process overlaid with information that is boring at best. Our goal for this book is to help students understand the convergence of roles (theirs and yours) in college choice and payment. We know not only because we've each worked in the world of college admission and financial aid for more than 40 years, but we've each coached our own children through the process—sometimes kicking and screaming.

There are more than 4,400 colleges and universities in the United States. This book will help your student find a great college, maybe one you've never even heard of, that will value her academic ability, talent, or special characteristics (embraces being green, a commitment to Amnesty International, or Ultimate Frisbee) and will *fund* her education. Really, that's how it works.

In the chapters of this book we detail the "what's" and "how's" and "why's" of the financial aid process in clear language that we hope will connect with students—and with you. We also describe a process for students to use to identify those colleges and universities that will fund their study, explain to them the realities of college costs, and suggest ways in which they begin the process and discussion with you about those costs and their management. A bonus chapter for parents is to help you begin and structure those awkward conversations about money for college and your own financial situation.

So: Buy this book, read it, have your student sit down and read it. You'll notice we not only directed the book to students but also wrote in language that will resonate with them—after all, when was the last time your student read something written to or for you? Never? Probably. We know you'll read and hopefully enjoy the language of the teen world. We had fun with it, maybe even periodically went a little over the top, but we're desperate to get their attention. Doing a college search the way we recommend will change their lives. Really, it will. For you, following our advice will help to keep you from assuming astronomic amounts of debt or to pay any more out of your pocket than is really, truly necessary to get your student a great education at a place that values her enough to pay her to attend.

This is how it works. We hope you enjoy the book, we hope it changes your student's life, and we can practically guarantee that if you and your student do things our way, you'll save money.

INTRODUCTION

To THE HIGH school students to whom we dedicate this book: There is a thought that may have already occurred to you. If not, it's coming soon. You'll think to yourself, "If only I had a disability." You'll look at your toes and think, "I could lose a toe."

If it would give you an edge in the college admission process, you would gladly lose a toe. That could be an interesting essay, you'll think. My life without toe(s).

Or, better yet: If only you were really, really poor; if only you were an orphan; if only you had survived cancer, or somehow overcome an enormous adversity like the "Homeless to Harvard" girl who, you think to yourself, *got into Harvard*. If only you had been a runaway, lived on a train, gotten an experience that could distinguish you, lost the aforementioned toe. You'll have a moment where you are actually jealous of your classmates who are in foster care or have children of their own or are physically disabled, of the kids who ran away from their abusive parents to live with a distant relative.

You might feel like a nerd, like a nothing, like a perfectly Plain Jane who has nothing interesting to offer, who has never taken any chances, who doesn't have anything to show for living a safe and middle-class life. You'll think you should have made some tragic problem for yourself and then risen above it in a demonstrable, essay-friendly manner. Sadly, you did not; you stayed home, went to school, did your homework, practiced the piano, and slowly, through time, morphed into the perfect candidate to get rejected from Amherst on the basis that "we have too many like her already." Or even worse, accepted—and then asked to take out a home mortgage's worth of loans to cover your tuition.

That might not sound worse to you, to get accepted at a little Ivy like Amherst. Worse, you think? How on earth could that possibly be worse than getting rejected? Getting rejected is humiliating, especially if one of your friends gets in. Your entire high school career has been filled, been overflowing, with people telling you that you should go to the best college you can possibly get into, that everything you do is important "for college," for "when you apply to college." Every single thing you do is something that "colleges like to see" or "colleges don't like to see."

College—and where people go to college—is where we, as a society, begin to separate the wheat from the chaff. Thanks to ratings boards, we can actually define colleges in a straight and linear hierarchy—good, better, best. People who go to Harvard and Yale are the smartest (how many times have you heard, "So-and-so went to Harvard, he's a really bright guy . . ."), and everyone else is slightly dumber than that. You want to go to the best school possible, because that is what everyone will approve of, and where you go to college affects the rest of your life—if you don't get into the right school, you won't be able to get a good job, and then you'll be poor and sad and dumb for the rest of your entire life.

Let's just say this: That kind of thinking is bananas. It is crazy. It is nuts. It makes no sense. Because here is the thing that is so important: College costs money. A lot of money.

We'll repeat it one more time: College costs a lot of money. Seriously, *a lot* of money. Anywhere between $100 and $250 *thousand* dollars. That's $100,000 to $250,000 with all of the zeroes attached.

With $250,000 you could buy, according to our expert Googling:

- One Lamborghini.
- A condo in suburban Boulder, Colorado (just one bedroom).
- A three-bedroom house in Idaho.
- 18 horses (trail horses).
- One racehorse (champion thoroughbred).

There is a secret to financial aid that no one has ever told you and probably never will tell you (at least before you graduate). Before we get into it, let us explain why: It is not a secret to anyone who truly understands capitalism. There is no secret admission and financial aid cabal, no Skull & Bones in underground meeting rooms. The secret, or rather the facts of financial aid, are simply a function of the American market. And when it comes to telling students, not only do the people who understand this assume that *you're* not smart enough to understand it, but colleges (and admission officers, and financial aid officers) *need* you to be ignorant of the fact, in order to drive up their application numbers, and thus increase their selectivity. This is both a function of your age, and the accessibility you likely have to at least two mid-career incomes (read: you are young, and therefore dumb, and your parents have more money than someone who is 25).

We'll try to describe this as simply as possible since you probably haven't had very much actual, on-the-ground experience with running a business (not because you're dumb, but because you're not really allowed to by law). Colleges gain income from tuition, from donors, from the U.S. government, and from endowments (the holding of wealth that they invest on the open market, in stocks, bonds, CDs, and other accounts). Money, in capitalism, essentially begets more money. Colleges improve their money-earning potential by climbing up a scale of selectivity, much in the same way one would assume that someone who graduates from Harvard would make more money (or have the opportunities to make more money) than someone who graduates from the local community college. Elitism and status beget more elitism and status, as colleges, through time, whittle their student body down to an Olympic-level pack of the best and the brightest.

Tuition dollars are used, essentially, as leverage to acquire the kind of students that a school wants in order to increase their status and selectivity. All tuition dollars forfeited (read: scholarships given to students) are dollars that must be spent by the college, and are only barely offset by the tuition payments made in full by non-scholarship students.

If this sounds cold, that's because . . . well . . . it is. Universities are businesses, just like everything else, not an altruistic force that exists solely to spread the "life of the mind." A university is not the secular, or non-religious, version of a church; it is much more like the intellectual equivalent of Google—millions of users, or consumers, whose needs and search terms dictate what the internet will produce. The more people Google "Katy Perry" or "Kylie Jenner," the more popular she becomes; the more students request programs like game design, the more schools will offer it, and the more that schools with proven employment for their graduates can attract students.

Universities, however, are not above their devotion to their product, that "life of the mind" we mentioned earlier. Just because it's not free doesn't mean it isn't there. There is, essentially, a hierarchy that holds the top schools (Ivies) above the almost-top schools ("Little" and "Public" Ivies) above a competitive upper-middle range of small privates, and then a solid middle range of publics and *really* small privates. Somewhere after the Ivies and Little Ivies are schools whose alumni are not so wealthy, and need to be enticed to donate with things besides status—for example, you might not get your name on the library, but you will be invited to a rock opera. And those schools are the creative and thoughtful places that are, you might say, actually less burdened by the status and selectivity needs of their alumni and students than colleges with more money than the country of Belgium. Those schools might have less stuff and less cash—for example, they may not pay to send you on spring break or give you a state-of-the-art gym in every single dorm—but nonetheless, they are wonderful places to learn and grow into an adult.

But why would you want to go to a place that has less stuff and less of a status name? The reason is simple: It's the important thing we told you about before: Money.

College costs a lot of money.

And chances are, you have neither a 4.0, perfect SATs and a hundred extracurriculars, or wealthy parents who can afford to shell out the entire cost of attendance. You are most likely an interesting person with pretty good grades and a family that might be doing okay, but not making a lot of money. Your family's income may not be low enough to qualify you (we're talking *really* low— under $30,000 a year for your entire household) for a huge need-based aid package. Chances are, you will have to take out loans, and under no circumstances will the name brand of your alma mater outweigh the burden of that debt. If you have a $700 monthly loan payment, *it does not matter where you went to college,* you will not be able to move to, say, New York City or Los Angeles, and take the unpaid internship you will *absolutely* need to get a better job. The world has changed. Very few employers hire people straight out of college with no work experience; there are simply too many people who have both a degree and relevant work experience under their belt at the age of 21.

So what does this mean for you? How can you take this information and get into college, much less pay for it?

This entire book is devoted to helping you answer that question. The first thing you need to do is understand that you may end up at a school you have never heard of; we're going to ask you to do research, and to expose yourself to the hundreds of marvelous schools who use the market to their advantage (read: will pay for you to be there, because they can and they want a student like you).

We need you to let go of all the crap everyone has thrown at you, let go of the status ambitions, let go of the ego, let go of the admission pressure. Let go of the voice in your head that says you won't get anywhere if you don't climb the social ladder. You're already doing great, just as you are. For starters, you're reading this book, which shows that you're already interested in taking responsibility for the events in your own life. You will become a successful and intellectually satisfied person in life, even if you don't go to your reach school. The world is an amazing and wonderful place, filled with problems to solve and abstract intellectual questions to ponder—at your job, on the subway, or playing cards with friends in a dimly lit kitchen, listening to music.

Life is an adventure and college has something to offer that no one can take away from you: It's the first time in your life when your life will really, truly be your own. It won't belong to anyone else—not your parents, not even your professors (after all, it's up to you to go to class). When you graduate from high school, the world will suddenly come into being, become yours to explore.

If you keep reading, and try to do what we ask, we promise that we will help you get into and pay for the right school for you, and graduate with a reasonable amount of debt.

This isn't a manual of academic tricks. We are explaining the market; this is not a game-the-system book, in the sense that we're going to teach you how to put one over on colleges and universities. Rather, we're giving you the tools to make an intelligent (and extraordinarily expensive) purchase in a market that will affect you after you graduate.

You might be wondering *why* we would tell you this. Will it affect our careers? Hardly—at least, we hope not. As an industry, we need to figure out a better way to run the business of higher education. Paying full tuition is not financially feasible for most of the people, and yet, the qualitative result of a college education is an invaluable experience of culture. A life in culture is a rich life, one steeped in awareness of the worlds of architecture, design, art, music, novels, history, politics, science, and ethics.

But at what price? How much is too much? We have an answer: Debt beyond $32,000. Because regardless of industry, independent lives are created first by financial security. You may tell yourself you can land a high-paying job after graduation—but what if you *don't want to*? Or what if the jobs are boring, or you're bad at them, or you're simply unlucky? The future is uncertain—and that is a wonderful thing.

We do know that going to college will enrich your life. The strongest future we can imagine is one built by patient, practical, and ethical college graduates. Without them—without the people who ask "Should I?" or "Is There a Better Way?" instead of "Can I?"—our world will turn into a sci-fi nightmare where technology is used for its worst purposes against a helpless proletariat of worker bees.

Okay, okay. We realize that *might* be a little dramatic. But what we're trying to tell you is that we care; we care about students individually, and we care very deeply about higher education. We've devoted our lives to it—more than 80 years between the two of us. And now, after all this time, we've decided to pass on what we know. No one else has gathered all the resources that we have between the covers of this book—and there's more on our website at thefinacialaidhandbook.com.

Grab a cup of coffee, settle down in your favorite chair, and please—*turn off your cell phone*. It's time to get real about college.

The 9 Biggest Myths About Paying for College

How DO YOU plan on paying for college?

If you're like most people, you will apply to five to 10 schools that you like, fill out your FAFSA, then cross your fingers and see who gives you the best offer. Then you will beg and plead with your parents, take out loans, and head off for college in the fall after your senior year. You may already have some idea of your family's finances; you're certainly going to apply for financial aid, if you've already picked up this book. Maybe you're planning on taking out some loans; but you'll figure all of it out *after* you have applied.

Perhaps you've *already* applied, and the FAFSA deadline is coming up—and you just want to know how to get the most money out of the government. *Hand over the tricks, ladies! Give me some charts and instructions and let's be done with it!*

Well, kid, we're sorry, but we can't do that. Like anything worth learning in college, you've got to listen to some old person drone on for a while. In your case, that "old person" is the two of us, Carol and Ruth.

If you've already applied to colleges, and you're just trying to use this book to figure out your FAFSA or apply for private scholarships, we have something terrible to tell you: You might not get a significant amount of aid.

The biggest scholarships and financial aid you can get—the kind that really matter—come from colleges themselves, and in order to get them, you've got to apply to the right kind of place. If it's already too late, and you're looking at taking on huge student loans, please turn immediately to Chapter 11. How much is *too* much to take out in student loans? Well, we consider anything more than $32,000 total, or $8,000 per year, to be unacceptable. (See Chapter 3 for more information about student loans.)

You might be thinking, *Why does it matter how much I pay for college? College is an* investment; *I'll be able to pay it back if I get a good job. And the better the college I go to, the better the job I'll be able to get.*

Unfortunately, that's not always true. But it's incredibly difficult to understand why that's not true; you are never given the opportunity to question it. *Socrates is a man; all men are mortal; therefore Socrates is mortal.* The more you pay for something, the more valuable it is; the more expensive the college, the better the education and the better the opportunities that follow. You've never been *asked* to question that kind of logic; it seems as natural as Socrates's conclusion that he is mortal. And you are an American teenager—going to college will happen no matter what. It's the new high school diploma. It is a foregone conclusion, an absolute must, a compulsory, mandatory event in your life. Here is your circumstance: You will turn 18, graduate from high school, and head off to college. Going to college does not feel like a choice. *But going to college, and where you go to college, is a choice.* The reason that it is a choice—and not mandatory—is because college is not free. It must be paid for. And because it must be paid for, you are a consumer, the same as someone selecting a new pair of jeans at the local mall.

When you think about colleges, there is a hierarchy in your brain of what is okay, what is pretty good, what is better, and what is best. There are a couple of assumptions you're going to make about college:

1. The more selective a college is, the better the college.
2. The more expensive the college is, the better the college.

These two things aren't necessarily true. You've got to question both of these assumptions.

We're going to spend the rest of this book explaining to you that much of what you *think* you know about colleges and universities is, in many ways, untrue. The most basic thing that we need you to understand is: Colleges are a business, and you are their target market.

This doesn't make you helpless. You're a consumer of education; you have the right to choose how you spend your money. The marketing of education, while intoxicating, is nowhere near as potent as tobacco marketing, for example. How many people have you met who are "addicted to learning" (other than scarily enthusiastic, middle-aged teachers with embroidered cat sweaters and "History is Fun!" pins)? Education marketing isn't nearly as potent, but nonetheless, the effect is the same: You and your peers are under the impression that the "better" the college you attend, the "better" the job you get will be.

This is reinforced by successful people with degrees from elite colleges—maybe you know them, or you read about them in the newspaper or in books or whatever. You might think that they're successful because of where they went to school, and that may be partially true. Going to school—any school—is important. A great education is extremely helpful in life, not in the least because it opens up your mind to all the possibilities of the world. But successful people are generally successful for two main reasons: First, they don't give up. Even when they fail, they pick themselves up and try something new. They are dogged and determined and have thick skins. And second, they're good at getting other people to trust them. Whether they are money managers, editors-in-chief, CEOs, or famous authors, they are trustworthy in some way or another.

Those are not qualities that one can purchase; those are personal traits that one earns, you might say, through a lifetime of hurling yourself into experiences and thinking, *life is an adventure in the great unknown*. No college can *teach* you that, although many, many colleges—easily 1,000 out of the 4,400 schools in the United States—will give you opportunities and experiences to figure that out on your own.

But again, college isn't free; colleges are businesses that need to charge you for their services. And their services are kind of strange. They're going to sell you a product (a diploma) that also comes with an experience (four years of reading and talking and studying). The idea is that the product (the diploma) will help you get a good, well-paying job, and that the experience (the four years of reading and talking and studying) is the cherry on top; at least, that is the easiest, most saleable idea.

The reality, of course, is that the brand name of the diploma has little to no value without the skills and experiences you have in the classroom. Those four years of reading and writing and talking and studying and failing and succeeding and picking yourself back up again and trying something new are what give you those two qualities of successful people: 1) you learn to persevere; and 2) you learn not to try and sell anything you don't really have (that is, you become trustworthy; you discover the value of integrity). But because that is nearly impossible to sell (and they can't guarantee that you'll come out with either quality), it's difficult to distill into a marketing campaign, into a slogan, or on to a brochure. And so colleges try to sell the diploma instead of the experience—to sell, in short, their brand.

Yes! Colleges have brand identities, just like the Swiffer sweeper, just like Mercedes-Benz, just like Bloomingdale's. They've all got a "brand" and an "identity" and they all spend a *lot* of money on marketing. All the images you have of "college" and "what college means" are part of the rhetoric, the intentional language, of college marketing. Ivy leaves crawling up brick walls; snowy-bearded professors spouting Keats to dreamy-eyed undergrads in perfectly preppy ensembles. That means sororities and fraternities; fresh notebooks and acceptance letters on linen paper; exclusive clubs and first-class tickets to the next echelon of society. College is the golden stamp of the upwardly mobile, just like cigarettes, once upon a time, were the hallmark of the teenage rebel.

You might think that colleges and tobacco companies are different, because tobacco is "evil" and learning is "good." But at the end of the day, they're not that different: They are selling a product. Just like someone standing in a deli waiting to buy a soda, magazine, or candy, when you shop for colleges you are the target of millions of dollars in marketing campaigns. Those campaigns are validated by rankings lists in the *U.S. News & World Report*. And it doesn't *seem* to be the same as soda or magazine or candy marketing because we, as a society, have accepted that learning is "good." And don't get us wrong—learning *is* good. But at what cost? At what point does paying for education become a bourgeois vice, a trap of socioeconomic vanity, instead of a legitimately useful thing?

When we published the first edition of this book in 2011, one of our favorite stories about the trap of higher education debt was in a *New York Times* article from May 29, 2010. Six years later, it is still important. In an article entitled "Placing the Blame as Students Are Buried in Debt," the paper profiled a recent graduate of New York University, a 26-year-old woman who took on just under $100,000 in private student loans in order to finance an undergraduate degree in women's and religious studies. Cortney Munna now makes $22 an hour as a photographer's assistant, a position that hardly requires a college degree. Her monthly payments, once she stops deferring them (she's currently taking night school classes for another degree), will be roughly $700 per month.

"I don't want to spend the rest of my life slaving away to pay for an education I got for four years and would happily give back," she said. "It feels wrong to me."

Well, of course she doesn't. But what prevented her from using basic algebra—the kind that a high school sophomore would understand—to determine how much her education was going to cost her?

The answer is simple: She was blinded by her perception of NYU's brand. She and her mother are both quoted in the article as stating that NYU was a "good" school, and because it was a "good" school, it was worth paying for with money they didn't have to spend. *Is* NYU a good school? It's certainly as good a place as any other well-funded research institution to get a good education. But the logic that is implied with "good" is that NYU's degree would help this young woman get a "good" job, a well-paying job, no matter what her chosen field of study. Does she have one? Absolutely not—at least not one that has anything at all to do with her college education. The job she has might be "good" in that it is intellectually and creatively stimulating, but it's not well-paying and she certainly didn't need a college degree to get it. And now, Ms. Munna will have to figure out how to make a $700-per-month loan payment, on top of her other bills (like rent, food, and transportation—easily $1,500 to 2,000 a month on their own). Forget about travel, about new clothes, about going out; Ms. Munna will have to make a base salary of at least $45,000 a year (if she wants to live on beans and rice) just to make her monthly bills.

Maybe Ms. Munna is a fluke, you might think—NYU *is* a good school. But how do you know that? If high graduate salaries mean that one school is "better" than another, then NYU fails; according to a recent PayScale.com study, the highest reported salary for NYU graduates is for students who became high school teachers, with an average annual salary of $49,151, making NYU's graduates solidly middle-class. Yet, NYU *costs* as much as Harvard, whose highest reported salaries for graduates in the same survey are for students who became CEOs and make between $99,159 and $287,152 per year.

That does, in a sense, make Harvard "worth" paying for—but not NYU, even though their cost of attendance is actually higher ($68,400 annually at NYU, versus $64,400 at Harvard).

So what does this tell us? Well, hopefully, you understand that while NYU might be a good place to get a good, or quality, education, it's certainly not a place that can calculate a significant return on investment, like Harvard does; in other words, NYU—and hundreds of other "good" schools just like them—cannot statistically demonstrate that their graduates make more money than graduates of many other schools.

There are about 25 colleges that can prove, year after year, that their graduates make a *lot* of money. Ever hear the phrase "starving engineer"? Yeah, us neither have we. Unsurprisingly, of the 25 schools that provide a significant return on investment, the majority are engineering schools and the remainder are Ivy Leagues and hyper competitive private schools. So if you're going to major in engineering, math, or one of the hard sciences—and you know you're going to be good at it and stick with it—then everything you already know about college probably *does* make sense. Go ahead and apply to the best engineering school you can get into; take out crazy loans and work your butt off. Statistically, you will likely be rewarded with a high-paying job. But as for the rest of you? Everyone who doesn't know what their major is going to be, or what they'll be doing in 10 years? Sorry, but you've got to keep reading. We've got 9 major myths about college to break down for you.

Myth #1: You get what you pay for

To be honest, when we started to come up with our myths, we could have gone on for hours. Heck, we could come up with a hundred—and not just about college. We can come up with money-myths for just about anything, but we wanted to keep it simple. So let's start with the simplest myth of all: that you "get what you pay for." You've surely heard that expression, which implies that cost, the *actual dollar cost of anything*, has a direct correlation to the value you're going to receive.

What does that mean? Well, it means that we live in a capitalist economy, with a system of exchange known as the "free market." The market is known as "free" because anyone, anywhere, can dictate the retail price for their own product. You might be familiar with Etsy, the online marketplace for handmade goods. Let's pretend Ruth has suddenly taken up knitting and decided to sell her chunky yarn scarves on Etsy. She can charge whatever she wants for them; in the free market, the government cannot step in and say, "Hey Ruth! The scarves you're selling on Etsy are too expensive. They should only cost $25." Ruth can go online and set up her page and charge $125 a scarf, if she so desires. She is "free" to set the cost of her goods at any number she likes, and neither the government nor the theoretical buyer of her scarves can do a darn thing about it. The only thing the consumer can do is not buy a scarf. So the consumer *can*, in essence, exert some kind of price control by *not buying any of Ruth's scarves.* After a week of no sales, Ruth might think, "Maybe these scarves are too darned expensive." And then, perhaps, she'll lower the price.

So the rules that govern the free market dictate that *demand* is the control mechanism of price; simply put, the market will not support a cost that is higher than the generally-agreed-upon value for any given thing. For example, this means that it's nigh-impossible to sell a Honda Civic, generally a $25,000 car, for $60,000, unless that Civic has some kind of additional value, like Taylor Swift drove it in a music video. But you'd still have to be willing to shell out another $40,000 for the privilege of driving to work in a "piece of history"; if you didn't care about Swift or music videos, you'd only have to pay $25,000 at any dealership in the country for *the same exact car.* The accepted value for that Honda Civic is $25,000, and presumably, a car whose basic cost is *always* $60,000—like a brand-new Mercedes-Benz—is going to be a "better" or "nicer" car.

And when it comes to college, value is a tricky thing. What do you get out of college, exactly? What is the primary reason to even go to college—other than the simple joy of learning? Is it to discover who you are? Is it to make friends? No. These are important, but they're much, much harder to put a price tag on. The point, to be blunt, is to get a good job. You want to go to college and come out on the other side with a good job, a better (that is, higher paying) job than you could get with just a high school diploma.

College graduates *do* make more money than people with just a high school diploma. On average, college graduates make $830,000 more throughout the course of their lifetimes, depending on who you ask.[1] But graduates from where? From what college?

If a college education has, on average, an additional lifetime value of $830,000, then it stands to reason that the "best" college educations have a larger lifetime value—more than $800,000 dollars. And what are the "best" colleges? What constitutes a school whose diploma can really, truly increase your earning potential?

The answer to that one is simple: The 25 or so colleges we mentioned earlier, the ones that provide the highest dollar amount of earnings beyond graduation, include four of the Ivy League colleges and a slew of engineering schools like Harvey Mudd, RPI, MIT, WPI, and CalTech. You can also throw in Rice, Stanford, UC Berkeley, Babson, and Carnegie Mellon, according to research by PayScale.com. The unfortunate thing about that particular list— which you can find online at their site and ours—is that it doesn't break down the numbers by major. But we can tell you flat-out that their data is likely heavily skewed by people who majored in math and the sciences: by engineers and bankers.

We'd like to tell you something about ourselves: We did not go to college thinking that we would make a lot of money someday. And we don't make a lot of money—but we do really, really love our jobs. Carol majored in literature at Macalester College in St. Paul, Minnesota, and Ruth majored in psychology and elementary education at Augsburg College in Minneapolis, Minnesota—both small, private liberal arts colleges that did not cost a lot of money at the time. Frankly, women of our generation were often expected to go to college to get our "Mrs." degree—to find a husband (we suppose that's another kind of "earning potential," albeit one with a single, stifling, uncreative goal). For us, making a lot of money wasn't something that women like us actively thought about doing, unless it was making out like a bandit in a divorce settlement. It wasn't something our mothers encouraged us or even expected us to do; although they expected us to know how to support ourselves, bringing home the bacon was not "women's work." And college was inexpensive enough that the idea of paying back student loans (neither of us had any) was of no concern to us. We wanted to go to college, get away from our parents, learn something, pierce our ears, grow our hair long, meet guys, and change who we were—that was the privilege of the 1970s. Did we "get what we paid for" back then? Absolutely. We learned as much as we could and we grew up. But what we paid in the early 1970s was *peanuts* compared to what college costs now, even though earnings for college graduates haven't risen significantly (about 1 percent per year) since 1975, the first year we entered the job market.[2]

Although your parents probably graduated at least a decade after we did, college costs didn't change as dramatically as they have in the last decade. In 1990, the average four-year private college charged $17,094 per academic year, and a four-year public college charged $3,492, on average (in today's dollars).[3] So just like us, your parents probably feel that they "got what they paid for"; the cost of college was not, for them, prohibitively expensive, and the idea that a more expensive college could provide a better education was much closer to the truth than it is now.

The cost of college has doubled since then. That same data set tells us that the average private four-year college now charges $32,405; the average public four-year college charges $9,410. That might sound low to you; it certainly sounds low to us. Based on our experiences with the private colleges we work for, we'd ballpark an average tuition figure somewhere around $38,000 per year, and public colleges closer to $16,000; looking at elite colleges (and pretenders to the elite throne) we would say the average high-end tuition is around $50,000 per year.

But how many people actually pay that full $16-, $38-, or even $50,000 dollars? What would you guess? Do you think everyone pays the same price?

They don't. Students and families pay wildly different prices to attend the same schools, take the exact same classes, and get the same diploma. And that's where the idea that "you get what you pay for" falls apart. If you can buy a car for $60,000—but everyone else is paying only $25,000 for it—does that make it more valuable? Absolutely not, and the same is true for college. If you pay an extra 10, 30, or even 100 thousand dollars more for your education, does that make it a better education? You can't re-sell your diploma, the bank can't repossess it, and you can't take out a loan on it; so why would you pay more than anyone else does? If you were really thinking about it, you would pay as little as you possibly could.

Cost, when it comes to college, is totally mutable—it is change-able and based solely on how much the college *thinks* you're willing or able to pay. This is a practice known as "tuition discounting"; it allows the college to change the price around for students they really want. Everybody does it—private colleges, big state schools, and even community colleges.

That means that if you apply to a college where you are in the top 25 percent of the incoming class, there is a *very* good chance that the advertised price—whatever they say on their website and admission materials about "how much it costs"—will be heavily discounted, just for you, regardless of your family's financial situa-tion. We would say, in our experience, that students who are in the top 25 percent of the incoming class almost always get a scholar-ship of some kind—frequently half-tuition or higher.

Myth #2: If you get into your reach school, you should go there

If the school you're dreaming of attending is a "reach" for you, then you *absolutely should not go there*, unless your family can afford to pay for it out of pocket. A "reach" school means that you'll be in the academic bottom of the incoming freshman class, and you won't get enough merit aid (a scholarship) to make up for the high cost of tuition. Essentially, when it comes to admission, the bottom half of the class pays for the top half of the class. Andrew Manshel, the former CFO for Barnard College, stated in an opinion piece for the *Wall Street Journal* on April 7, 2010, that colleges charge as much as they do *because they can*: "There are qualified paying custom-ers lined up at the door." And who is the most willing to pay that price? The student or parent who never dreamed that little Fanny or Freddy was "good enough" to get into an elite, or *perceived elite*, school. Fanny and Freddy are the most susceptible consumers for the college, the ones who are willing to take on loans and sell property in order to move up a level, in order to "be accepted" by what they perceive as a place that is "better" than who they already are.

And from the college's perspective? Why admit students who aren't as "good" as the other students? Truth be told, Fanny or Freddy was admitted to the reach school solely because the school predicted that the student's family would be so thrilled that they'd move mountains just to pay full price. When Fanny or Freddy—or anyone else in the bottom of the incoming class, who can define their acceptance into that college as a "reach"—are accepted, the school can then turn around and offer an enhanced scholarship to a Maxine or Martin who have incredible test scores, through-the-roof-recommendations, and are being vied for by 12 other colleges. Fanny and Freddy have the money for tuition, but Maxine and Martin have the statistical advantages that will help the college move up in the ratings to secure more Fannies and Freddies who will pay more to be at a "better" school. Both kinds of students provide income to the college: Fannies and Freddies through direct payment of tuition, and Maxine and Martin as Fanny-and-Freddy bait. Believe us, you'd much rather be a Maxine than a Fanny: Maxine doesn't pay a lot, and Fanny does.

This might not make any sense to you. But an important thing to know about tuition costs is that they are often determined on an entirely different balance sheet from the rest of university costs; in other words, how much a college costs does not directly reflect how much it costs the college to enroll a student. Tuition and overhead are, in essence, often very different things, and actual tuition—the real price of college—is determined on a student-by-student basis. *Your tuition costs are all about how much the college thinks they have to discount (or not discount, in many cases) the sticker price in order to get you, your money, or your grades, to go there.*

Our friend Jon McGee, who works at Saint John's University and the College of Saint Benedict in Minnesota, has a wonderful phrase he uses to explain college tuition to friends and family. Jon says, "In no other business can someone ask, 'How much does it cost?' and the response is, 'Well, give me a copy of your tax return and a transcript, and I'll let you know.'"

That process is of enormous value to colleges; it allows them to learn all about you before they determine whether or not they're going to admit you, and for how much.

From now on, you're not going to use the words *safety* and *reach*. Those words are bad. Wipe them from your consciousness. There are two new words on the horizon: *funded* and *unfunded*.

You're going to start, right now, thinking about college the exact same way that people think about graduate school: Where can you get funded? It's no longer about getting in—it's about getting funded. For graduate school, there's no shame in going to whatever school will fund you; prospective graduate students will tell you that they'd rather go to the University of Illinois or the University of Minnesota as funded students than to Harvard as unfunded students. And now, all 4,400 of the degree-granting colleges and universities in the United States are going to part like the Red Sea into two categories in your mind: "funded" and "unfunded." There is no more "safety"; there is no more "reach." Now there are only two kinds of schools: the kind that will fund you and give you a sizeable scholarship, and the kind that won't.

Promise us that you will not go, under any circumstances, to an unfunded school. Let's make a pact here and now to only *apply* to schools that you can think of as "funded." Why should you promise us that? Well, this book is called *The Financial Aid Handbook*. If you were rolling in dough, you wouldn't have bought it; you wouldn't be reading this paragraph right now. You'd be out on a yacht in St. Tropez, throwing gold Krugerrands in the air—well, maybe you would still be in high school, but you wouldn't be thinking about how to pay for college.

We know what you've been told. You're supposed to go to the best college that you can get into—go to your reach school, if you can get in. Then, after you get in, you're supposed to figure out how to pay for it. But that is backward: to that, young man or woman, we say *no way*. You're going to figure out what schools will fund you—and then you'll apply.

Myth #3: I'll wait until *after* I'm accepted to figure out how to pay

For as long as we've been working in college admission (more than 80 years between the two of us), students have started the college search by finding schools they *could* love—and then falling *crazy* in love with one final choice. The standard college application cycle is about 22 months long; it begins when you take the PSAT as a junior, then ends when you set foot on campus almost two years later. After you take the PSAT, you'll get all sorts of colorful brochures in the mail, and get bombarded with emails, too. Those mailers scream, "Look at us! Love us! We're the college for you!"

You're getting those brochures in the mail because of your test scores. The colleges sending you these multicolored, high-resolution love letters have looked at your scores and determined that you're a likely candidate for admission—that you've got, at the very least, the lowest test scores they're willing to accept. Despite what you might think, those colleges don't have *any* access to information about your family's financial situation; they have no idea if you are capable of paying to go there or not. To be frank, they don't *want* to know—colleges don't generally want to shock you by talking about money (how gauche!). Colleges want to lure you in with the perfect first date (or campus visit); they want *you* to fall in love with *them*. As to whether or not they'll love you back, that remains to be seen— after you've applied and sent in your transcripts and FAFSA. At that point, you've splayed yourself upon the altar of love; you've declared, "I love you, college." And that's when you're the most vulnerable— when you're desperate to be loved back. That's the moment when you're most likely to say to yourself, "I didn't get a scholarship, but it's only $30,000 in loans per year . . . that's worth it, right?"

Let's go back to what our friend Jon says about college tuition: "In no other business can someone ask, 'How much does it cost?' and the response is, 'Well, give me a copy of your tax return and a transcript, and I'll let you know.'"

It's true. Can you think of any other product that requires you to submit to an in-depth review before you can purchase it? Other than country club memberships and co-op apartment buildings, there are virtually no other products (you're buying it, so education is a product) in which someone gets to extensively review and judge you before you're allowed to buy. It's kind of a humiliating thing, if you think about it; the retailer (the college) gets to know all about you, your hopes and dreams, and the last four years of your life and your parents' assets, before they will even *deign* to tell you how much their product (your education) will cost you.

And that process of reviewing you, of holding power over you, is how colleges get you to the point at which you say, "It's only $20,000 in loans per year." And then you become a Cortney Munna—someone with all the best intentions and tons of debt, yet without a job.

Before you apply, though, it *is* possible to predict how much each school is going to charge you by analyzing yourself the same way that colleges and universities do. That process is detailed in our Merit Aid Profile, or MAP, in Chapter 6.

You've also got to figure out how much you and your family can afford to pay; after you do that, you can find schools you like, determine whether or not you have a good chance of getting funded there, and then, finally, visit and apply.

Myth #4: If my parents say they won't pay, I'll get more aid

There are lots of word-of-mouth stories that become persistent urban myths. Someone hears from someone that *so-and-so got more money from a school because the parents wouldn't fill out the FAFSA*; or *so-and-so became legally independent (legally emancipated) from the family and got a full scholarship.*

Unfortunately, these stories are almost always just that—stories. One of the fundamental tenets of financial aid, which is funded and supported by the U.S. government and its taxpayers, is that your parents are fully responsible for your college education. The FAFSA is used to determine how much money your family has available to pay for college. Simply because your parents don't *want* to pay does not excuse them from the responsibility to do so. In order for your family to be absolved of all responsibility to pay, you would have to qualify as an independent. To qualify, you would have to meet at least one of the following criteria:

- Be 24 years of age or older by December 31 of the award year.
- Be an orphan (both parents deceased), ward of the court, in foster care, or previously a ward of the court when 13 years or older.
- Be a veteran of the Armed Forces of the United States or serving on active duty for other than training purposes.
- Be a graduate or professional student.
- Be a married individual.
- Have legal dependents other than a spouse.
- Be an emancipated minor or in legal guardianship.
- Be a homeless youth.
- Be a student for whom a financial aid administrator makes a documented determination of independence by reason of other unusual circumstances.

If you are an unaccompanied/homeless youth, please skip ahead to Chapter 15. Mark this page and return to it later. If any of these other points describe you, you can be treated as an independent student. If not, your parents must fill out the FAFSA in order for you to receive any aid.

In some circumstances—especially with divorce and blended families—one or more of your parents may absolutely refuse to pay or provide you with their financial information. If this is the case, see Chapter 4.

If your parents are reading this with you right now, please make sure they read the following paragraph:

Parents:

When you graduated from high school, you may have been able to make your way through the world without a college diploma. That is no longer the case. If you've brought children into this world, you have the responsibility to help them through it. That doesn't mean they have to go to the most expensive college (if you've read even *one page* of our book so far, you'll know we'd never advocate for that), but it does mean that in order for them to receive any financial aid, you must fill out the FAFSA and help your child in any way you can. College is not only a wonderful experience, but it has become as necessary as high school. Please don't let your own experiences in the world allow you to make judgments about what your children should or should not have. Please trust us when we say that they ought to go to college for many good and sound reasons, and if you don't at least help them by filling out the FAFSA, the federal government won't be able to give your child *any aid at all*. You will be punishing your child and handicapping them financially if you do not fill out the FAFSA (or PROFILE). For more information, take a look at Chapter 5, written just for you.

Whew. There, we've said it. If your parents aren't convinced by our pleas, turn to Chapter 4 and try some of our other tactics.

Myth #5: Only the very poorest will get any financial aid

You don't have to be poor to get financial aid. The popular press often focuses only on the Pell Grant program (which generally gives grants to low-income students) whenever "financial aid" is mentioned; this leads many, many students to believe that "financial aid" is only for poor people. But the Pell Grant isn't the only form of financial aid that comes out of the FAFSA or PROFILE; there are numerous kinds of grants (money you never have to pay back), loans (money you do have to pay back), and work-study (money you earn while in school) that you become eligible for by filling out the FAFSA or PROFILE.

We'll give you more detail later in Chapter 2, but for now, here is the bare-bones statistics on how your eligibility for financial aid is determined.

The FAFSA is the Free Application for Federal Student Aid. It's a series of forms you fill out (in print, or online) that details your parent's assets—their income, their savings, dependents (including older relatives), and the number of children that will attend college. It also details your (the student's) income and assets (although you probably don't have much). All the numbers you put down get crunched through a standard formula that determines something called your expected family contribution, or your EFC. The EFC is the amount of money in actual cash that your family is expected to contribute each year (anywhere from $0 to $999,999), and filling out your FAFSA also makes you eligible for federal fixed-rate student loans. You can also get a loan from a bank at a high interest rate—but that's a terrible idea. Turn to Chapter 3 for more about loans and debt.

Most recipients of Pell Grants have a household income of under $50,000 annually, but the more children or dependents your family has, the less the actual income amount matters. Although it's not common, families with incomes of more than $100,000 per year *do* receive the Pell Grant and other forms of need-based aid;[4] it just depends on how your family has to spend their money. According to the federal government's FAFSA calculation, taking care of an elderly relative is a reasonable expenditure that lowers your EFC, but making payments on a yacht is not; same with sending four kids to college (low EFC) versus buying four new cars (high EFC).

The best thing about the FAFSA is the FAFSA4caster, which allows you to estimate what your EFC will be, anytime you want—even if you're in seventh or eighth grade. This helps to give families a realistic starting place for the discussion about college costs, and we think it's one of the smartest things the Department of Education has ever done. It's online and it takes just about 30 minutes. Go to fafsa4caster.ed.gov to fill it out!

There's another way to understand how much you might have to pay: Each college or university has on its website a net price calculator, or NPC, as required by the federal government. NPCs can be good (really helpful and specific, giving both merit- and need-based aid estimates); bad (adding in loan amounts so that it appears as if your cost will be zero); or even ugly (using only a federal template that gives averages by income bands). Ultimately, NPCs are only really valuable once you have a "consideration set," or a group of colleges in which you are extremely interested.

Myth #6: I can pay someone to find scholarships for me

Anyone who charges you to find scholarships is scamming you. They're taking advantage of your fear, your youth, and your parents' desire to get you into college. The practice of charging for scholarships has become so egregious that the Department of Education has multiple warnings on its website.

However, there is an enormous amount of free information out there about private scholarships (the kind you find on lists, websites, or in books at your library); we're big fans of FastWeb (full disclosure: Ruth used to be on the board), a free online service that will match you to scholarships that are a good fit (and sometimes to school-specific scholarships). Please check our website, thefinancialaidhandbook.com, for an index of helpful scholarship resources.

The confusing thing about "scholarships" is that the word has two uses: one is for "private" scholarships, the kind you can read about on the internet or in books. Private scholarships come from Coca-Cola, the 4-H Club, the Bertha Carruthers Institute for Proper Young Ladies, and the Doug Douggleston Memorial Golf Foundation. They come from veterans organizations, the PTA, and your local Gambler's Anonymous club; they come from anywhere and anyone. But where they *don't* come from are individual colleges.

The second use of the word *scholarship* is for the other kind, the kind that comes only from the college. They're known as "institutional" scholarships, or *merit aid*. You're going to read the words *merit aid* a lot in this book—get used to it! Merit aid only comes from the college itself, and you become eligible simply by applying. Merit aid is the same as tuition discounting, it's the same as an institutional scholarship, and it's part of—gasp!—financial aid.

We know. It's confusing. But essentially, merit aid is never adver-tised in books or on websites other than the college's own. To find out about what kind of merit aid is available at the college of your choice, you'll have to do some research. We cover this in Chapter 6.

Never, ever pay for scholarships—and limit the amount of time you spend applying to private scholarships. It can be a huge drain of your time and energy, and although all of those books on the shelf at Barnes & Noble tell you there are "Thousands of schol-arships inside!!!" and "Billions of dollars in free money!!!" what they neglect to tell you is that there are currently 20.5 million col-lege students in the United States, and many of them are applying for the exact same scholarships. If you're going to spend time and energy sending off scholarship application after scholarship appli-cation, be judicious about it and use a free service like FastWeb or Cappex.com to narrow down the best options.

Myth #7: My state school will be the cheapest for me

Other than tuition, the basic costs of education—room and board, books, travel, and other expenses—are generally the same at any kind of school, be they public or private. Unless you plan on living at home, you won't be saving much on anything except tuition, and even then, you may not save much.

The main problem with public universities is their graduation rates; the chances of graduating in four years are significantly higher at a private school. Public schools often have unwieldy core curricula that make it difficult to change majors (which stu-dents almost always do), and your chances of graduating in five years—instead of four—at a public are nearly 50 percent.[5] It's best to graduate in four years, if you can; otherwise you lose two or more years on the job market (or hey, bumming around Europe, or teaching English in Japan).

Although the average cost of tuition at a public university is about one-third the average cost of tuition at a private school, your chances of getting a scholarship are generally slimmer. We're not saying that you *shouldn't* apply to your local state school (we think you should!), but it can't be the *only* place you apply. There are plenty of private colleges that will welcome you into their open arms and discount their tuition (ahem, we mean give you a merit aid scholarship) enough to be quite competitive with your local public college.

Myth #8: College will soon be free

And we have a bridge in Brooklyn we want you to buy. We know that during the 2016 presidential campaigns, promises were made to provide free tuition at public colleges and universities. Yet, a rough estimate marks this cost at $75 billion per year,[6] funding that would still need to be passed by a federal congress. Fifty separate state legislatures in turn would have to commit to matching agendas of reinvestment and reform. Though it is an admirable plan, we are not confident in our government's ability to enact it.

But some governments have accomplished this, you might be thinking. *Sweden has free college, so if Sweden has it, why can't we?* Well, the Swedish government picks up the tab, and in order to do so, they have to collect taxes to pay the bill. That is expensive; Sweden has an effective personal tax rate of almost 57 percent, which means that for every dollar (or krona) Swedish parents earn, the first 57 cents goes to the government, leaving 43 cents for things like food, a place to live, a car to drive, and clothes to wear. And though tuition is free, Swedish students still have to live somewhere, eat, buy personal stuff and books, and maybe even have the occasional beer. The result, even with "free" college, is the average student loan debt in Sweden is more than $19,000. Eighty-five percent of Swedes graduate with that debt, as compared to 50 percent in the United States, where our current average tax burden is 31.5 percent, according to a 2015 report from the OECD.

Raising taxes so significantly is a complex process. Any plan for "free college" would have to be a sweeping bipartisan effort to convince both Republican and Democratic lawmakers to raise taxes significantly, and our current political climate does not indicate that sweeping bipartisan efforts are likely or even possible.

However, we are still optimists. Check back with us in 2021 for the third edition of this book—maybe it'll be a different picture! For now, if you are going to college in the next five years, don't bank on "free" college as your personal finance plan.

Myth #9: I'll get money from colleges by joining a "funding scheme"

A funding scheme like Raise.me certainly sounds like a good idea. Students take a survey, revealing their extracurriculars, achievements, clubs, sports, and volunteer activities, and colleges simply *give* away scholarship money in return—all thanks to a selfless team of revolutionary social entrepreneurs in San Francisco.

Surprise: It's not selfless, it's not revolutionary, and these are not new or even necessarily personalized scholarship dollars, no matter how they are labeled; this type of "funding" is simply a new way for colleges to collect data on prospective students using the tuition discounting that they already practice (and have been practicing for decades) as scholarship-flavored bait.

Essentially, colleges want to know who you are early in your college search so they can market to you. That isn't really a bad thing. The colleges would have given you that money anyway as part of your need-based grant, assuming you demonstrate the need on your FAFSA at their college. You really only get *more* money (and not a lot) if you *don't* qualify for need-based grants at their school.

It's entirely possible that the colleges participating in Raise. me or other similar websites may not be schools you would have looked at, and may be perfect for you, or they may be not good for you at all (you can assess them using our MAP in Chapter 6), but whatever they are, they have paid Raise.me to get your information, and in turn, Raise.me may take some information back. As of this writing, that includes your enrollment and graduation information, which could mean your grades and alumni addresses. They also reserve the right to share that information with anyone they do business with.

Our biggest complaint about websites like this is simple: the enormous amount of time and energy required to submit your data. There is a human being who can provide all of these services for you with a few short conversations, and that person is your high school college counselor (and they won't sell your address to Arby's).

That's all for myths, folks. We hope you've enjoyed this eye-opening trek into the world of college admission and tuition! And if you didn't, we sincerely hope that it has been at least useful. For the advanced (or more literal-minded) among you, our next chapter concerns the basic nuts and bolts of financial aid. If you're just beginning to learn about money and don't care to bore yourself with the details just yet, please turn to Chapter 3, where we talk about student loans, debt, and life after graduation.

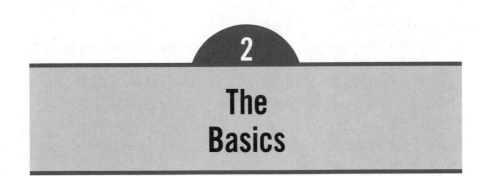

2

The Basics

No MATTER WHERE you're thinking about going to college, you should apply for financial aid. You might not think that you "need" financial aid, or suspect you're not eligible for it—but you absolutely should apply for it anyway.

The cornerstone of every financial aid process is the Free Application for Federal Student Aid, or FAFSA. It's the very first thing you fill out, and you'll have to fill it out each year while you're in school. The FAFSA determines your "need," or how much your family should pay for college. Your "need" has two components:

1. How much your family should pay in actual cash each year, also known as your "expected family contribution," or EFC.
2. Whether or not you're eligible for federally funded grants (money you don't have to pay back) or loans (money you *do* have to pay back).

You can file the FAFSA as soon as October 1 of the year before you will go to college. For those parents who have recently sent another kid to school, you'll recognize a change. The Federal Government changed the date and considers the previous calendar year's taxes so that, given you've filed, you can use the Data Retrieval Tool (DRT) to autofill your tax information. Read on and we'll tell you more.

The FAFSA is provided by the U.S. Department of Education, part of the federal government. We didn't always have the FAFSA; your parents may not have used it, because it only came into being in 1992.

You might wonder, "Why do we even have financial aid?" Furthermore, "Who is paying for me to go to college? Why would they do that? What do they gain? Why is the government involved in what is often a private enterprise? And what is 'need?'"

Need: noun. A necessary duty, or obligation; a lack of something requisite, desirable, or useful; a condition requiring supply or relief; or the lack of the means of subsistence (poverty).

In your case, "need" is your lack of something requisite, desirable, or useful: money. But how do colleges define "need"? How do they determine who needs money, and who doesn't? You might think that it's a simple process, but for such a tiny word, with such a seemingly simple definition, it manages to confuse nearly everyone who is wondering how to finance a college education.

You might think that colleges define "need" with a simple set of definitions—with a chart, perhaps. That chart you're thinking of might look something like this:

Income Level	Financial Aid Award
Lower-lower income	Full tuition
Middle-lower income	$25k per year
Upper-lower income	$20k per year
Lower-middle income	$15k per year
Middle-middle income	$10k per year
Upper-middle income	$5k per year
Lower-upper income	Bupkis
Middle-upper income	We're insulted you even asked
Upper-upper income	Yes, colleges will take gold bricks in payment

Unfortunately, we made that chart up. No such chart exists; if there was such a thing, you wouldn't need this book, and we'd be out of a job.

So if colleges aren't using a chart like that, how do they do it? Is it consistent? Who makes the guidelines?

Well, defining "need" happens on a case-by-case, or individual basis, taking into account your financial information, your grades, and sometimes your demographic information. But because finances are complicated, there is an overarching set of guidelines, or a methodology, that defines *how* we define "need." That's the FAFSA.

Need Dictionary: The top 27 words and phrases you "need" to know

FAFSA: The Free Application for Federal Student Aid is the form you fill out to share your financial information with colleges, so they can determine how much you can afford to pay. The FAFSA's federal methodology determines your EFC, and the results are forwarded to your choice of colleges. You may file for the FAFSA on October 1 of the year before you plan on enrolling in college. That means if I want to go to Ruth's Pretty Good College in the fall of 2018, I'll submit my FAFSA on October 1 of 2017. FAFSA is a noun, in case you were wondering, but you may also use it as a shorthand verb (Have you FAFSA'ed?) by conjugating it in the usual manner. You will use the Data Retrieval Tool to submit your 2016 tax information. FAFSA is available at FAFSA.ed.gov.

EFC (Expected Family Contribution): This is the amount of money that you, and your family, are expected to spend on your college education, annually, as calculated by the federal methodology used in the FAFSA.

COA (Cost of Attendance): Every college and university calculates its own cost of attendance, which includes tuition, fees, housing, food, books, personal supplies, and transportation. This is also called a "budget" when calculating your financial aid package; the college will subtract your EFC from the COA to arrive at your "need."

NPC (Net Price Calculator): All colleges and universities are required, by the federal government, to display a Net Price Calculator, or NPC, on their website. The calculator must provide cost of attendance and grant and scholarship aid, broken down by EFC range, housing type, and tuition.

FAFSA4caster: We *love* FAFSA4caster. This is a quick (30 minutes or so) "pretend FAFSA" that you can use online at fafsa4caster.ed.gov, anytime, day or night, to get a good idea of what your EFC will be in the months and even years (if your household income is consistent) leading up to October of your senior year of high school.

CSS PROFILE: The FAFSA is free—but the PROFILE is not. It costs $25 for the first college, and $16 for each subsequent college. It's often required from students by colleges that want to determine how they hand out non-federal money (read: the college's own funds) to students, and it is a much more detailed form than the FAFSA. It requires both parents, custodial and non-custodial, to fill it out; it takes into account home equity, and it's tied to the consumer price index, which the FAFSA is not. The CSS PROFILE is administered by a private nonprofit, the College Board. To access the PROFILE and for a list of colleges that require or accept it, go to bigfuture.collegeboard.org. Most schools require financial aid applicants to file the Profile if they are applying early decision.

Methodology: This simply means "formula," as in all the formulas you learned in algebra. The "federal methodology" is the FAFSA system for taking the financial data from everyone who wants to apply for financial aid, and using a standardized system—a methodology—to determine how much discretionary income they have for education. An "Institutional Methodology" is used in the PROFILE.

Institution: Colleges love this word. This does not mean a mental hospital, prison, or sanitarium. *Institution* refers simply to any one body of post-secondary education (after high school). An institution can be a community college, a private college, a university, or a trade school. They're all defined by the Department of

Education as "Higher Education Institutions," or HEIs for short. When a college is giving its own money for a scholarship or grant, that money is called "institutional money" to distinguish it from that which comes from state or federal governments, or any other outside scholarship organization.

Dependents: Anyone who depends on your parents, including you. This is a frequently misunderstood question in the FAFSA. Count yourself as a dependent. You will likely be claimed as a dependent through all four years of college by your parents, even though you may file your own taxes.

Dependency Status: There is a worksheet to determine whether or not your parents can legally claim you as a dependent. It's not just a matter of declaring yourself independent—you have to pass a series of online tests at fafsa.ed.gov. Things such as age, marital status, military employment, or level of education determine whether or not you are an independent. If you are an 18 year old who is unmarried, not in the military, and living in your parent's house, you are probably dependent.

SAR (Student Aid Report): The Student Aid Report is the document (either paper or electronic) that lists the information you've reported on your FAFSA. Your EFC will be in the upper right-hand corner of the front page. This is the form that gets sent out to colleges.

FSA ID: An FSA ID is a username and password that you must use to log into certain U.S. Department of Education websites, like the FAFSA site. To sign the FAFSA electronically, your custodial parent should also apply for an individual FSA ID. The FSA ID is used to sign legally binding documents, *so do not give your FSA ID to anyone!* Apply for an FSA ID at studentaid.ed.gov.

PIN: The PIN was replaced by the FSA ID on May 10, 2015. Demonstrating a rare sense of humor, the U.S. Department of Education wrote an obituary for the PIN on its official blog. You can read the obit (and sign up for a FSA ID) at bit.ly/2ehxUPz.

Student Aid Eligibility: The period of time for which you are eligible for student aid, loans, or grants, from the federal government. Your student loan eligibility can be removed if you have, or acquire, a felony drug conviction.

Loan: Any amount of money you borrow and then have to repay. Loans have interest, or a percentage of the total amount that you have to pay additionally to the holder of your loan. No one hands out money for nothing; for example, on a $10,000 loan at 3.76 percent interest (the federal rate; a private bank will likely charge more), expect to repay a total of $12,036, or an additional $2,036 on a 10-year term.

Term: The amount of time you have to repay a loan.

Parent: Who is considered a parent? Well, your biological, adopted, or stepparents are; but grandparents, foster parents, legal guardians, older siblings, uncles, or aunts are *not* considered parents unless they have legally adopted you. If your parents are divorced, the parent you have lived with most in the last 12 months is considered your parent for the purposes of the FAFSA. For PROFILE, both parents—custodial and non-custodial—will have to fill out forms. *If your divorced or widowed custodial parent has remarried, you must also provide information about their spouse on the FAFSA and PROFILE.* So, a note to parents who are looking to remarry: If you remarry, you will take on the financial burden of educating your new spouse's children, and they yours, in the eyes of the federal government. These are modern times. If you're not ready to unite your lives both emotionally *and financially*, please think long and hard about living in sin and what it can do for your pocketbook. This is in no way unethical—it is important for you to understand that although marriage can have its benefits, it can also have its federally determined flaws.

School Code: This is a six-character number code for each college or university that you want to receive your FAFSA information. Search for it on the FAFSA website at fafsa.ed.gov. Be forewarned: If you misspell the name of the school, you won't find it. This may be confusing because it's not "College Code," but the federal government uses "School" for both K-12 and higher education institutions.

DRN (Data Release Number): This is the four-digit number that will be assigned to your individual FAFSA. It's on the upper right-hand corner of your electronic SAR, printed on your paper SAR, and also appears on your confirmation page. This number gives you access to all of your FAFSA information, so don't give it to anyone that you don't want to see your FAFSA. You'll need this number to change your permanent mailing address, email address, telephone school number codes, or housing plans.

Signature Page: If you don't use an FSA ID to sign your FAFSA electronically, you (and your parents if you're a dependent) will have to physically sign, with pen and ink, a signature page and send it off in the mail. The address to which you will send it is printed on the signature page. Just as when you sign with an FSA ID, you agree to the following conditions from the U.S. Department of Education:

- You will use federal student aid funds received during the award year covered by this application solely for educational expenses related to attendance during that year at the institution of higher education that determined eligibility for those funds.
- You are not in default on a federal educational loan, or have repaid or made satisfactory arrangements to repay the loan if you are in default.
- You do not owe an overpayment on a federal educational grant, or you have made satisfactory arrangements to repay that overpayment.
- You will notify your school if you do owe an overpayment or are in default.
- You understand that the Secretary of Education has the authority to verify income reported on this application with the Internal Revenue Service and other federal agencies.

If you purposely give false or misleading information, you may be fined $20,000, sent to prison, or both.

IRS DRT (Data Retrieval Tool): Yes, you read that correctly— the IRS is a part of this process too! Their Data Retrieval Tool (DRT) allows you and your parents to prefill portions of the FAFSA by accessing tax return information from the IRS and transferring it to the FAFSA. This is way cool and reduces errors—or as financial aid people think of them. . .

Database Mismatches, or "Flags": When you complete the FAFSA, you need to follow the directions word for word and complete all the information carefully and correctly. Some of the information on the FAFSA is cross-referenced with other federal databases, such as your Social Security Number, name, and birth date; these need to match your Social Security records. Even though I might like to go by "Carolita Stack," my given name is Carol Ann Stack, so if I were filing the FAFSA, Carol Ann Stack would be the name on the form. If there is a "database mismatch," your application will be flagged for correction and verification. This slows everything down, so be extra careful and double-check every piece of info on your FAFSA.

Confirmation Number: Even though you might think that having a DRN, an SSN, and a transaction number is enough, the federal government disagrees with you. The last page of FAFSA on the web will include a confirmation page, with—you guessed it—a confirmation number. They don't tell you how you might need to use it, but they do ask you to keep it for your records, just in case. And hey, you're keeping track of all the other numbers anyway—what's one more to add to the list?

Verification: Like any good moneylender, the federal government reserves the right to verify, or double-check the truthfulness of, the information you've put in your FAFSA. It can also require colleges and universities to double-check your information before anyone hands you a dime. So don't lie.

FAA (Financial Aid Administrator): Not the Federal Aviation Administration, but the designation for the Financial Aid Administrator at your college of choice. They're responsible for awarding aid and for ensuring compliance with state and federal regulations—in short, they're in charge. Never tick off your FAA; never try to bribe them, either. This is a person with whom you may have a good many conversations in the years to come (especially if you come from a non-traditional household with multiple divorces, children, and so on), so try to be cool with them.

Supplemental or Institutional Application: A form designed by individual colleges to collect additional financial information. It's free for the student and different at every school. Not all schools require this.

FAFSA Transaction: Every time you file a FAFSA, or make corrections to your existing FAFSA, it's referred to as a "transaction," and a "transaction number" and new SAR are created. So, when you speak with the financial aid office at your school, staff may refer to a change you made in "transaction 3" or "transaction 5."

Defining need, one more time

At the beginning of the chapter, we couldn't define "need" beyond the dictionary definition. We said it is on a case-by-case basis. And that's still true, but now that you've so thoughtfully and thoroughly read our Need Dictionary, you'll understand when we say that defining actual need happens by:

Taking a college's COA, or Cost of Attendance, and subtracting your EFC.

That means, for example, if Carol's Pretty Good College has a COA of $45,000 (which includes tuition, books, housing, transportation, personal supplies, and so on), and the FAFSA determines Ruth's EFC to be $10,000, then Ruth's need is $45,000 – $10,000 = $35,000. This is how much Ruth can conceivably get from the federal government and the college itself in both loans and grants.

But, bear in mind that actual need can be $35,000 at one college, and only $15,000 at another. Actual need changes based on the COA of the college in question.

Let's pretend that Carol's husband David opens up a college of his own. He decides to charge less than his beautiful wife does. So, at David's Wonderful College for Young People, the COA is $35,000;

Ruth's EFC, as determined by the FAFSA, is still $10,000. So Ruth's "actual need" at David's Wonderful College for Young People is $35,000 – $10,000 = $25,000. That's how much the college could conceivably help her get in federal loans and grants.

Even though the "actual need" changes, the EFC is still $10,000, and that number is difficult to change or adjust. Whatever your EFC is determined to be is how much your family *should* be paying in cash annually, but that number often sounds extremely high to families. That's where "perceived need" comes in: Your parents may think that you have more need than you actually do, based on their spending habits. Often, families have more in debt than they do in assets. Consumer debt—things like car payments, mortgages, and credit card debt—won't take your family off the hook when calculating your EFC. The federal methodology simply looks at how much money you have coming in, *not how you spend it*. Many families look at their EFC and think, "How am I going to come up with that kind of money? What am I supposed to do, sell my house?"

Well, you could take out a home equity loan, or you could start changing your lifestyle. We cover ways to do that in Chapter 5. The EFC is not an unreasonable formula, as much as it might seem to be. Keep reading, and we'll explain it more in-depth.

The expected family contribution: Let's get (right) down to the real nitty-gritty

Although Gladys Knight and her Pips never attended college, we bet that if confronted with the EFC, they would have broken out into "Nitty-Gritty" right there in the financial aid office and demanded some answers. Don't get the Gladys Knight reference? Well, your parents will. They'd probably like to read this chapter, too, so once you're done with it, hand it over to them.

How on earth do they calculate the EFC? Gosh, Gladys, we're so glad you asked. Well, for a dependent student, which 99.9 percent of you high school students are, there are two components to the EFC:

1. The parent's contribution from income and from assets.
2. The student's contribution from income and from assets.

For starters, all the financial information used is from what's known as the "base year," or the taxable year that precedes enrollment. This is also known as "prior prior year." Yes, you read that correctly—prior modified by prior. For a student starting college in the fall of 2018, the base year would be 2016. To calculate the parental contribution from income, first the methodology takes account of the taxable income earned in the base year, and adds directly to that the amount of untaxed income earned in the base year. All of this information has been reported on your FAFSA. Then, any income that can be excluded is subtracted; that includes education tax credits, child support, certain kinds of earnings received by the parent (if the parent is a student, for example, and earned federal work study funding). The final number is the parent's total income for the base year.

From the total income, allowances are subtracted for:

- Paid federal income tax.
- State and other taxes.
- Social Security Tax (FICA).
- An "Income Protection Allowance." Known as the IPA, this accounts for basic living expenses needed to maintain the family as a whole. The IPA recognizes that certain expenses must be met before a family can even begin to think about paying for college. The IPA is a benchmark (read: set number) based on an income level below which a household is assumed to have *no* discretionary income (read: extra spending money). The amount of the allowance, which varies by family size and number of children enrolled in college, is adjusted each year according to changes in the Consumer Price Index. The IPA has the following breakdown:

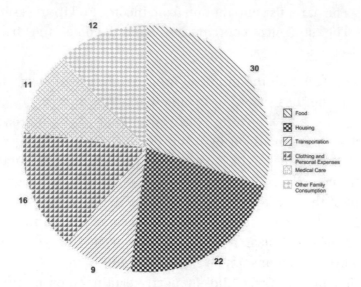

The IPA is helpful, but it's not a huge amount. For a family of four, with one child in college, the income protection allowance is $27,440 (for the 2015–2016 fiscal year). That's not very much.

There's also a subtraction for employment expenses; that allowance is 35 percent of the lesser of the two *earned incomes* (if there are two working parents), or of the *earned income* of a single parent, capped at $4,000. Earned income is important; it's not the same as a taxable asset. So, on to assets we go!

Assets

The calculation of your parents' total assets is again taken from information that you've reported on your FAFSA. The information used to calculate this is:

- Cash, checking, and savings.
- Net worth of current investments. This includes real estate (but *not* the family's primary residence), trust funds, money market accounts, certificates of deposit,

stocks, stock options, bonds, 529 plans, commodities, and more.

- Net worth of a business or investment farm, unless it has 100 or fewer employees.

All of those things are added together, and then an education savings and asset protection allowance is deducted from this to protect the parents' assets. You might be thinking, "What would they want to spend money on besides my college education?" Well, there are a lot of things: retirement, emergencies, other family members, education for themselves or any siblings you might have, that busted water heater, turning your room into a gym, and so on.

After the education saving and asset protection allowance is deducted, the remainder is considered to be a "discretionary net worth," or an amount of liquid cash ripe for the spending. However, not all of it is assumed to be available for education; a 12 percent asset conversion rate is applied to the discretionary net worth, and that finally results in your parent's contribution from assets. If the number is negative, it's reset to zero.

At last. We've calculated both the contribution from income and the contribution from assets. After this, the process starts over with the student's income and assets. The process is essentially the same, except for a few important differences:

- The Income Protection Allowance for the student is set at $6,400.
- No adjustment is made to the net worth of a dependent's business or farm (this means that putting shell corporations in the name of your children to hide your own assets *will not* help you).
- There is no asset protection allowance for a student's assets.
- The contribution is assessed at a flat rate of 20 percent (no sliding scale).

The student contribution is the sum that comes from adding the student's income and assets. The EFC, or expected family contribution, is the sum of the parents' contribution and the student's contribution. There is, however, a simplified version of the EFC that disregards assets. A dependent student qualifies for this simplified calculation if:

- The parent's combined adjusted gross income (or income earned from work) was less than $50,000 and either:
  - The parents were *not* required to file an IRS form 1040.
  - One of them is a dislocated worker, as defined in the Workforce Investment Act of 1988.
  - Anyone counted in their household size received a means-tested federal benefit, such as welfare.

There's also an automatic zero EFC (yes, you read that right—an automatic zero, as in no dollars) if, and only if:
- The parents' combined adjusted gross income (or combined income earned from work) is $25,000 or less and either:
  - The parents were *not* required to file an IRS form 1040.
  - One of them is a dislocated worker, as defined in the Workforce Investment Act of 1988.
  - Anyone counted in their household size received a means-tested federal benefit, such as welfare, during any of the three previous years.

You've probably heard about the zero EFC before—it's often known as a "full ride." But kids, here is the thing: If you suspect that you qualify for an EFC of zero, *you still have to fill out the FAFSA correctly and on time*. If you don't do that, colleges won't be able to help you. If your parents can't help you fill out the form, contact your school's guidance counselor and say that you suspect you qualify for a zero EFC and that you'd like help in filling out the FAFSA. They should set aside at least an hour, and possibly make a home visit, to make sure that you get the form filled out correctly.

There's nothing embarrassing or wrong about asking for help, and we've noticed often in households that do qualify for a zero EFC, the parents are usually working multiple jobs or working at night. They simply don't have the time to help you figure this out, so asking a guidance counselor is a great way to get it done without causing discord at home between you and your already-stressed parent(s).

What does all of this tell you?

Well, it means that we've tried to create a formula to assess need, but, as with any other formula, in many ways it's pretty arbitrary. Although the final analysis is probably pretty darn good at separating those with no ability to pay (zero EFC) from those with a great capability to pay (an EFC of greater than $90,000), it isn't particularly good about the shades of grey in between, where most families fall. And although it might seem tempting to shift assets from a parent to a child to try and hide those funds from the government, in the end, the asset rate—up to 12 percent for parents and a set 20 percent for children—makes shifting assets (read: moving money around) a lose-lose.

You will likely fall into the middle, into a grey area, where your EFC doesn't compute and you don't think you can live up to paying it outright. The lower your EFC, the higher your aid award from any given college. Although there are a number of strategies out there for adjusting your EFC (pushing taxable income into the next fiscal year, for example), in the end, it won't make much difference. Pushing income into the next year will only come back and bite you in the rear when you fill out the FAFSA again (yes, you have to fill it out every year), so the best thing to do is to look at your spending and try to adjust. For extenuating circumstances—for example, if one or both of your parents recently lost their jobs, you'll have to negotiate directly with the aid office. You can't appeal your EFC, but you can explain it to the Financial Aid Administrator (FAA) at your college of choice.

For a good idea of what your EFC will be, use the FAFSA forecaster in the months or years leading up to October 1 of your senior year. It's online at fafsa4caster.ed.gov, and it's a great way to start planning for your college costs during your sophomore and junior years (if you expect income to remain consistent).

The CSS PROFILE

You may have to fill out the CSS PROFILE, which is administered by The College Board (a private organization) in addition to the FAFSA. Why? It seems crazy! What else do they want from you? How many times can you possibly write out your social security number and calculate your income? Well, just like the government, colleges are stingy about giving away their money, and in many cases—especially with divorced families—it's easier to hide assets from the FAFSA than it is from the PROFILE.

A quick note for all you students with Deadbeat Dads and Moms: If one of your parents is punishing the other by denying you financial support for your college education, and *has the means to pay for your education* (read: has money), the PROFILE may not be your friend. The PROFILE requires both custodial *and* non-custodial parents to submit their financial information; the FAFSA only requires the parent you reside with the most to fill it out. So if you have one wealthy parent, who you don't live with and who is refusing to pay for your education, and he or she fills out the PROFILE, your aid award from the college will *not* be consistent with your EFC. It'll be much lower than it would be if you only turned in a FAFSA. So if you have a Deadbeat Dad or Mom (and parents, you know who you are), contact each college you're applying to that requires the PROFILE and request a waiver of non-custodial information. It'll be painful, and you'll have to spell out exactly what is so disharmonious about your family life to a total stranger over the phone, but financially, it's worth it. Dry your tears, because if you have a Deadbeat Dad or Mom and you're attending a school that requires the PROFILE, you might have to do this annually.

On a personal experience note, this is actually pretty common. During our careers, we've handed out countless tissues and had hundreds of phone calls with students who were in a sticky divorce situation and didn't know what to do. They were embarrassed, hurt, and confused, but they were all pretty pleased to discover that the colleges we worked for (and every single college or university you will apply to) had a protocol for Deadbeat Dads and Moms. It's ugly and it's hurtful, but it's a common thing, and you can't adjust your aid award or get the non-custodial form waived unless you contact the financial aid office at the colleges you're applying to and simply lay it all out there.

Let's get back to a basic explanation of the PROFILE. The PROFILE takes into account the equity of the home you live in. Colleges that use the PROFILE often make assumptions or demands that the FAFSA does not; for example, they may ask each family to have an additional contribution from assets based on the family's home equity situation, or expect from each student a summer earning contribution of a specified amount. It's different at every school, so if you have already narrowed down your list, and you know for sure that some of those schools require the PROFILE, request from their financial aid office an explanation of how they use the PROFILE to determine aid. This might be a helpful way to anticipate your aid award. Why is this helpful? Because it may be that the college in which you are the most interested assumes each student will have $3,500 from summer earnings or that the family will be able to obtain financing from home equity. Knowing what the assumptions from the college are will mean that you will be able to consider, and counter, when the time comes.

The PROFILE is an online form that can be found at bigfuture .collegeboard.org.

After the EFC: need-aware and need-blind

When it comes to need, colleges and universities fall into one of two categories: need-aware and need-blind. Let's start off with need-blind, the more common of the two need categories.

The Ivies, and other schools with buckets of money, describe themselves as "need-blind" and say that they "promise to meet full need." This means that they can admit anyone who fits their academic profile, regardless of their ability to pay, and that they'll meet the student's full demonstrated need. Translation: They'll pay for the gap between your COA and EFC.

Three important things about these schools: They have very large endowments, they have an incredibly strong brand presence in the market (which means they might be a "reach," or "unfunded" for you), and their students have out-of-this-world academic credentials. A typical student admitted to a need-blind school that meets full need has high test scores, a high GPA, speaks multiple languages, plays two instruments, lettered in multiple sports, and makes Mother Teresa look like Mr. Burns when it comes to community service. Statistically, there's only one thing that correlates with all of those attributes: family income. The wealthier your parents, the more likely you are to score high (thanks to extra tutoring), play sports (costly equipment and time), and volunteer (no need to work after school for money)—so when you break down the incoming freshman class of most need-blind schools, there really isn't much economic diversity there.

Another permutation of need-blind is to be need-blind for admission, but not to meet the full need of everyone who applied for assistance (or to meet that need in different packages for different students). This is often called "admit-deny"; admit to the college, but deny for full aid. This can get kind of ugly, but not all schools have the money to fund everyone, or they may offer aid packages that are less attractive to some students. This approach is fairly common. At Carol's Pretty Good College, for example, we really value students who are in the top 10 percent of their graduating class. So, we award our aid on a "matrix basis" (many colleges publish their matrices—something we talk about in Chapter 6— which is what you'll use to search for your match), where a student in the top 10 percent of his or her class will get a need-based aid package with a higher percentage of his or her need met with "Gift Assistance" (a merit aid scholarship), than a student who is only in the top 25 percent of his or her class. Students of lesser value to the college will get packages that have more loans and work, and less scholarship money, or they may not get any institutional money (merit aid) at all. Remember: You can have need, and still get a package of the state and federal funds you might be entitled to, but it won't meet your full need—it won't fund you.

Need-aware is the other kind of admission policy; it means that if you apply, and you can't afford to pay and they don't care to fund you, they won't bother admitting you. It sounds unethical, but it's not—from their perspective, why admit-deny? What's the point? If they genuinely don't think that you have the money to pay, and they can't find an excuse to pay for you—either a financial excuse (you really can't afford it) or a merit excuse (you're a star and they want you)—why waste your time with an offer of acceptance? This is an important thing to remember when you start to get your acceptances and rejections in the mail. You might have been qualified for entrance to a certain college, but if they really didn't think you could or would pay, then you didn't get admitted. It also helps to explain why some of your classmates with weaker credentials could be admitted to places you weren't: They simply might have more money. It's unfair, and it stinks, but at least you don't have to feel rejected on the basis of your academic credentials alone.

Everyone's individual aid offer is, at the end of the day, unique. There's no *always* when it comes to aid; there's just "more likely" and "less likely." That's why in Chapter 6, we put so much emphasis on doing the research—you've already come up with a list of schools that match your credentials and put you in the "more likely" category, before you've even applied. If you get accepted, it's up to you to compare your offers and eventually figure out the right place for you (which, in an ideal universe, is a college where you'd love to go).

The Gap

Finally, we come to the crux of the need issue: the Gap. No matter where you get in, there's likely going to be a gap between the merit aid offer you get from the school and what you still have to pay out. The Gap looks like this:

1. COA – EFC = Actual Need.
2. Actual Need – Aid Offer From the College of Your Choice
   = The Gap.

If you can't pay your full EFC, you can also add the difference between the full EFC and the amount you can actually pay (known as your Actual EFC) to the Gap, which brings you to the total amount of money you have to come up with. If that math looks weird to you, or you don't understand it, try making a quick worksheet that looks like this:

Direct Costs	College A	College B
Tuition	22,000	17,000
Fees	150	2,500
Room and Board	8,500	9,500
TOTAL COSTS	30,650	29,000
Scholarships/Grants	12,000	8,000
Balance	17,650	21,000
Your EFC (use fafsa4caster)	10,000	10,000
The Gap	7,650	11,000

The ideal college is one that has the smallest possible Gap, and the best emotional and intellectual fit. In the previous scenario described, College A wins out, by a neat $3,350 per year, or $13,400 over four years. Please note that Scholarships/Grants do not include work study or loans.

How are you supposed to fill the Gap?

You'll fill the Gap with grants (money you don't have to repay, if you're eligible), federal student loans, work-study, and need-based and/or merit-based aid. We get into student loans extensively in the next chapter, but our rule for student debt is simple: Don't take on more than $32,000 total in loans, or roughly $8K per year, in student loan debt—federal loans, never private. If your loans exceed that, you might not be able to pay them back and live the life you'd like to. To think about it another way, don't take on more in loans than you expect to make your first year out of college. According to the National Association of Colleges and Employers, 2016 starting salaries for college grads will range from $34,891 (education majors) to $64,891 (engineering majors). The Project on Student Debt (ticas.org), a nonprofit independent research and policy group (and as smart and thoughtful an organization as we've ever seen) considers the national average in 2014, the most recent year for which such data is available, of $28,950 in student debt to be too high. We think it's best to err on the side of caution. So keep your loans as low as you can.

Grants

Grants are wonderful. Take as many of those as you possibly can. They can come from the state government, federal government, or non-governmental sources and you never have to pay them back.

PELL GRANTS

Pell Grants are probably one of the most well-known federal grant programs. They originated in 1972 as the "Basic Educational Opportunity Grant Program" but were renamed for Senator Clayton Pell of Rhode Island in 1980. Pell Grants are targeted to the neediest of the college-going population. *Both U.S. citizens and eligible non-citizens can receive a Pell Grant.* For information about Pell Grant eligibility, go to studentaid.ed.gov.

Pell is a pretty large program, awarding roughly $30 billion dollars annually in grants to more than 8.2 million students. In general, to receive a Pell Grant, you must have an EFC of less than $5,234. The best thing about Pell is that it's an "entitlement" grant; that means it's yours to take with you no matter where you want to study. The maximum annual award for a Pell Grant is, as of publication, $5,815 per student per year. The FAFSA will determine whether or not you're eligible for a Pell.

SUPPLEMENTAL EDUCATIONAL OPPORTUNITY GRANTS

Supplemental Educational Opportunity Grants (SEOG) can come from the federal government. Like Pell Grants, SEOGs go to the neediest students, generally students with an EFC of $4,500 or lower. The very neediest students (likely those with an EFC of 0) will be considered *first* for SEOGs. The primary difference between SEOGs and Pell Grants is that a Pell gets paid directly to you, but an SEOG will go directly to your school, which is required to give it to you, either by crediting your account, paying you directly, or both, at least twice per academic year. The maximum SEOG is $4,000 per student, per year. SEOGs have been routinely underfunded in recent years, so they generally go only to the very neediest students.

TEACH GRANTS

If you're already a junior or senior in college and you're looking for more federal grants, check out the TEACH grant. TEACH grants are for students who agree to teach full-time in schools that serve low-income students for at least four of the eight years following graduation. Basically, if you know you're going to teach in either an underserved population or subject, or both, a TEACH grant will net you roughly $4,000 per year. If you don't teach, it reverts to a low-interest loan. For more information, go to studentaid.ed.gov. Note that the TEACH program was affected by sequestration (the automatic federal budget cuts of fall 2015), and funds may still be limited in years to come.

STATE GRANTS

State grants are generally only awarded to students who are going to stay *within* that state for college; in other words, Minnesota will not give Minnesota State grant money to a student who goes to study in California. But not all states have a large variety of options for your college education; Wyoming, Alaska, and New Mexico all have limited numbers of colleges and have some grant monies that may be taken out of state for qualified applicants. State grant awards vary widely; for example, the Cal Grant award was

$9,223 for tuition and fees for a student who attends a private college in California, while the "Access Missouri Grant" has a maximum of $2,850 for students who wish to study at private colleges in Missouri. For an extended list of state grants and more, please visit our website at thefinancialaidhandbook.com.

Work-study

At most colleges, students with need are usually awarded a work-study contract. This is, besides grants, probably our favorite kind of financial aid. Work-study means that you have to work an on-campus job—like baking muffins in the cafeteria, working at the campus coffee shop, or shelving books in the library—in order to earn your money. After you've earned it, it's yours to do with what you want. Generally, a work-study award is about $3,000 per year, which means roughly 10 to 12 hours of work per week. On-campus work-study jobs are awesome. What other employer allows you to schedule your work around your classes, wear whatever you want, and hang out with your classmates at the same time? You don't have to commute, because you're working on campus, and you don't need any work experience at all to get a work-study job (although experience can sometimes help you choose what job to do). The biggest benefit of all is a statistical one: Research over the years has shown that students who work 10 to 12 hours per week on campus are more likely to be successful.[1] That's because with a work-study job, you spend time with another set of adults, professors, or mentors, outside of class, who are interested in your ongoing success. If you've already gone through the application and aid process and you *haven't* been awarded work-study, call your financial aid office and ask how you can get an on-campus job, or ask if they can reduce your loan amount with work-study.

Student loans

Really, the only student loans you should ever become familiar with are federal Direct loans. Also known as the William D. Ford

Direct Loan Program, Direct loans are administered completely by the federal government. The amount you can borrow depends on your year in school (freshman, sophomore, and so on), and in some ways, your need as determined by the FAFSA. Direct loans fall into two types.

DIRECT SUBSIDIZED LOANS

Also known as "sub" loans, a subsidized loan is one for which the government pays the interest on the loan while you're still in school and for six months after you graduate. If you take on a sub Direct loan after July 1, 2016, the interest rate will be fixed at 3.76 percent. That's a great interest rate. There are, however, limits to how many sub loans you can take out: $3,500 your freshman year, $4,500 your sophomore year, and $5,500 in each of your junior and senior years. If you're going to take out that much each year, do so in *only* sub loans, if possible; they're the absolute cheapest loans you can get. You do not need a cosigner for a Direct sub loan.

DIRECT UNSUBSIDIZED LOANS

Also known as "unsub" loans, an unsubsidized loan is where the government doesn't pay the interest on the loan while you're in school. The loan will accrue interest from the very first day you take it out. Unsub loans are generally more expensive, because they carry an extra four (or more) years of interest. Unlike sub loans, the limits aren't staggered: You can take out up to $2,000 in unsub loans any year that you're in school—freshman, sophomore, junior, or senior. If your parents don't qualify for a PLUS loan (a kind of student loan for parents), you may take out up to $6,000 in unsub loans each year that you're enrolled in college.

The maximum amount of money you can take out in federal loans is $31,000. Our absolute maximum amount of *reasonable* student debt is $32,000; that gives you an extra $1,000 in wiggle room for credit-card debt, a state-based student loan or a Perkins, or, in an absolute pinch, a private loan.

STATE LOANS

Some states offer student loans that are accessible for both state residents attending colleges out of state and for non-residents coming in-state; the Minnesota SELF loan is a good example. Minnesota SELF offers something that private loans can't; there are no origination, guarantee, or processing fees, and it has a limit of up to $20,000 per year. But because it's not a state or federally guaranteed loan, it often requires a cosigner (just like a private loan), and the payment of interest while the borrower (you) is in school. They also have both fixed and variable interest rates (meaning that the interest can go up or change with the market). State loans, like private loans, are best only for real emergencies.

PRIVATE LOANS

Private loans come from banks and other lenders. Banks such as Wells Fargo, Citizens Bank, TD Bank, and almost any other bank in the country offer student loans, as do Discover and Sallie Mae. Do not be confused by banks: They don't lend money to students because they're interested in helping you go to college. Banks want to make money off of you, plain and simple. They'll also try to paint federal loans as *bad*. If you go to a student loan or aid fair, they'll be there, handing out free popcorn, tote bags, or some such other swag to try and get your attention. Private loans are the most expensive kind you can take out, and generally a terrible idea. We hate private loans so much we could literally fill an entire book about them with horrible stories, but that wouldn't be very helpful. So here are the basics: When you take out a private loan, there are as many possible kinds of fees as there are colors in the spectrum, just like a mortgage or a car payment. Banks have no interest at all in lending money to you, someone with no employment or credit history, for a product they can never repossess. What would they do with your diploma? Put it on their wall? They can't do anything with it. The only real incentive is that it is very difficult for you to have these loans discharged (read: eliminated) through bankruptcy. Interest rates on private loans are high, and they vary with the market. If you miss a payment, something bad will inevitably happen: Your credit will be affected, you'll get an extremely high fee tacked on, or, worst-case scenario, you could find that your debt has *actually doubled*. You'll also need a cosigner, so if you don't pay them back, you'll drag your cosigner into the muck with you. Most private loans aren't insured against death or disability, either; that means if you die, or get into a horrific accident, your family will be stuck with your student loans in addition to your medical bills. We explain this more in-depth in the next chapter, but the bottom line is: Do not take out private student loans. Ever.

If you don't follow our advice, and you take on a private loan, pay it off as fast as possible, and prioritize it the same way you would for any other high-interest debt.

Scholarships

MERIT AID

We touched briefly on merit aid, also known as "scholarships," "gift aid," or "tuition discounting," in Chapter 1. Merit aid will be your best friend when it comes to filling the Gap, but you won't find out what your merit aid award is until *after* you've applied. (For more information about predicting your merit aid award, turn to Chapter 6, where we cover the basics of understanding your likelihood of receiving a scholarship.) Merit aid comes from the college itself; in other words, it's their own money. Merit aid often goes to the students who have the highest test scores, class rank, GPA, or community involvement (academic, extracurricular, athletic, or community leaders) of the incoming freshman class. That means at a school where your stats are *just good enough* to get you in the door, you won't get any merit aid, but at a school where you're the best and the brightest, you'll get half-tuition or more. Unlike need-based aid, colleges can give out merit aid to whomever they please; after all, it's their own cash. For sample merit aid awards, our Merit Aid Profile (MAP), more information about merit aid, and tuition discounting, turn to Chapter 6.

TALENT-BASED SCHOLARSHIPS

Talent-based colleges and universities are far from cultural wastelands. Instead, they reward talent *as well as* academics—music and theatre nerds, Quiz Bowl stars, debaters, and many other kinds of special talents that they reward with scholarships, *if* that talent is important to the college or university. That "if" can be really important: *If*, for example, a school with a Scottish heritage has a bagpipe band on campus, then having that band at school events—homecoming, alumni weekend, graduation, and so on—is a big priority. What do you need for a proper Scottish band? Bagpipe players! So odds are, that school has a "talent award" to reward and recruit bagpipe players, but they don't care a fig for students who play in a drum and bugle corps.

ATHLETIC SCHOLARSHIPS

If you're skilled enough in any given sport that your coach or athletic trainer has encouraged you to apply to a DI or DII school, go directly to the ncaa.org eligibility center online. Never, ever pay anyone to find an athletic scholarship for you; just like someone trying to sell you a bridge in Brooklyn, or an "inheritance" in Nigeria, anyone who charges for a scholarship is scamming you. *The Athletic Recruiting and Scholarship Guide* is a great resource for students and parents who are looking for an athletic scholarship. However, if you're just someone who loves to play—and plays well—DIII schools might be a better fit for you. But you won't get an athletic scholarship at a DIII school; they cannot and do not give athletic scholarships.

So how much financial aid can I get?

If you've read all of this straight through—without flipping to other chapters, forgetting about this book entirely, or pulling your hair out—we salute you. This is where it gets *really* complicated, because it's different at every single school.

Our hard-and-fast rule for aid is this: *If you're in the top 25 percent of applicants, you'll get the most need- and merit-based aid possible.* Different schools all have different amounts of money to give out, so your offers may vary from place to place. But if you're in the top 25 percent, you'll likely get the best package that particular college can give. So if you really need those aid dollars, don't waste your time applying to colleges where you fall in the bottom 50 percent; you may get *some* aid, but it won't be enough.

So for each school that you like—and that you think will fund you—you'll fill out our MAP chart (or heck, make your own—just copy it from Chapter 6) and determine the likelihood of receiving enough in aid (grants, loans, need-based, and merit-based aid) to fill the Gap. And once you've decided on a school, applied, and been accepted, you'll have to fill out the FAFSA again every single year. And the better you understand the language, the formulas, and the structure of financial aid, the higher your chances of being able to effectively negotiate your financial aid awards in the coming years. So although this chapter might have bored you to tears (or worse, scared the pants off of you), it's time to celebrate because the worst is over. This was absolutely the most foreign and confusing part of the book, and now you've got an incredible wealth of financial aid knowledge under your belt. It'll benefit you in the next four years and if/when you apply to graduate school. It's time to dog-ear the page, grab a soda, pass this chapter off to your parents, and go sit outside with your friends for an afternoon. Promise us you won't talk about college for even a minute.

Let's Talk
About Debt

WHO ARE YOU going to be when you graduate from college? It's nearly impossible to know the answer. You might be interested in becoming a veterinarian; you might become a CPA; maybe you'll be chaining yourself to hundred-year-old redwoods and fighting for the rights of our planet. Whatever it is, you want who you are—essentially how you define yourself—to be about the things you do, about what you're interested in.

The magnificent freedom of a college education will allow you to decide that for yourself. You'll be able to learn about all avenues of life, and dream up scenarios of yourself walking down them—in a sharp suit, clutching a pair of drumsticks, wielding a paintbrush, or climbing a mountain. Trust us: You will want, and will love, to walk or *run* down those avenues. And the only thing that will hold you back are your student loans.

You can choose how to live after you graduate. If you want to spend your money on a fancy apartment, go ahead; if you want to share a house with eight other people so that you can go skiing every weekend, you can do that too. You can have a cell phone (or not). You can have a TV (or not). You can choose how to spend your money in every single way except for one: your student loan payments.

When you take out student loans, you are agreeing to make a monthly payment for the next 10 or 20 years after you graduate from college—anywhere from $50 to $1,000 per month or more.

There's no two ways about it: Taking out a student loan means agreeing to a monthly payment that begins right after you graduate.

Your monthly student loan payments are something you'll choose well before you graduate from college—you will choose them the *instant* that you decide what college to go to, when you decide how much you'll need to borrow each year in order to graduate. The total amount you will borrow, on a particular loan term (either 10 or 20 years; we recommend 10), will be broken down into monthly payments, scheduled for the next 10 to 20 years after you graduate, from the moment you sign off on your first Direct loan.

Now, there's nothing *wrong* with taking out student loans; in fact, we encourage it. Taking on a reasonable amount of what is known as "good debt" can be a very positive thing; it will raise your credit score and further enable you to take on other loans (for graduate school or a house) later in life. And from your family's perspective, it's *your* education—you should be responsible to pay for as much of it as you can. You've probably assumed, as well, that you are absolutely going to take out loans. Most of your friends will. But how much do you really know about loans? How much do you know about borrowing? Unless you've had a credit card that you're responsible for paying, we bet you don't know very much at all. And student loans are something you shouldn't walk into blindly, assuming that no matter how much you take out, it will pay off in the end. You need to think hard about it, do the math, plan for the future (in the worst-case, lowest-paying job scenario possible), and *then* take out a loan.

How much you will take on in student loans is *not* a mystery to be solved after you graduate. You will know, unequivocally, from the very first day of college, how much your monthly payments and total debt will be. Student loans, unlike a mortgage or a car loan, cannot be dissolved in bankruptcy. In fact, one of the few ways to get rid of them entirely (without paying them off, of course) is through *death*. Student loans will have, quite literally, a death grip on you.

This might seem incredibly unfair. Why can someone buy a million-dollar house with money they don't have, and then get let off the hook in bankruptcy? You're borrowing for your *education*. It is not a Jaguar convertible, it is not a private plane, it is not a frivolous purchase. It is something that you genuinely need in order to move forward in life. So why are student loans so difficult to discharge?

A great deal of the difference lies in what you're purchasing: education. Let's start with the concept of *equity*. When you think about purchasing a house or a car with money you don't have, the bank that lends the money to you sees the house or the car as something called "equity," which means the actual dollar value of the property. If you default on your loan payments for your mansion, yacht, or helicopter, the bank that loaned you the money to buy them in the first place becomes the actual owner. It can repossess—and most importantly, *resell*—the mansion, yacht, or helicopter at any time. What on earth would a bank do with your college diploma? The lender can't do anything with it; it's illegal to sell on eBay and the college certainly won't buy it back. It is of literally no value to anyone except *you*. So the lender—in this case the federal government—*does* have a vested interest in helping you repay the loan. The lender, in the case of what we'll call "educational equity," does the only thing they can to help you out: They keep interest rates low and promise not to change (or "adjust," in the insidious language of banking) them before the end of the loan term (the last day you have to pay it back— 10 or 20 years into the future).

The other major problem with student loans is, quite frankly, *you*. What incentive does a bank possibly have to give tens of thousands of dollars, for the purchase of something it can never repossess or resell, to someone with no credit history or employment record? The bank has no guarantee, at all, that you'll repay the loan (other than a general statistical likelihood that college graduates have jobs). For actual banks—private lenders such as U.S. Bank and Wells Fargo—the problem of *you* is the biggest problem of all. Private banks will not only require a cosigner with a good credit history, but they'll keep your interest rates sky-high at 10 percent or more. We'll cover this again later, but student loans from private banks—from anyone except the federal government's Direct loan program—are a total rip off that is absolutely, shamelessly designed to take your money. Never, ever take them out unless it is the only way you can finish your last semester of college and get your degree. If you do, have a plan to pay this off first, quickly, and with alacrity! Choose the cheapest government repayment plan you can and put your money against the more expensive loan.

Even federal loans can have their drawbacks if you take out too many, or don't plan for the future—if you don't think about how much it's going to cost you from *day one*. If you're not careful, your student loans will be the only thing that defines you; they can severely limit how you can live and what you can do with your life.

Debt even affects people who don't want to make a lot of money or don't care about making a lot of money. In fact, it often affects them the most.

Let's look back at an example of a real person we interviewed for the first edition of this book whose life has been completely altered by his student debt.

Gray, a 35-year-old painter who lives in New York, attended a private arts college on and off for several years in his early 20s. He now lives under an assumed name in an attempt to avoid his student loan debt of roughly $66,000, which, thanks to mounting interest, grows larger each year. Gray lives in a tenement-style apartment building with a month-to-month lease; his credit rating has been destroyed by his inability to repay his student loans, so the prospect of finding a nicer (or safer) place to live is impossible without using someone else's real name on a credit check or lease application. His cellphone is registered under a girlfriend's name. He is currently unemployed; if he were to get a job using his real name, his wages would likely be garnished each month by a collection agency.

When Gray first started attending art school, he received financial help from his parents and, with their encouragement, took on loans. Although he presumably signed the student loan equivalent of a promissory note—something that says "I know I have to pay this back,"—he doesn't remember it, or even seriously thinking about repayment. The math, he says, was optimistic:

> I wasn't concerned about [repayment] when I took out the loans. I mean, all my friends were paying like $160 a month for their loans, and I [thought] okay, that's doable. My rent at that time was $450, I sell one painting a month, I had a $20-per-hour part-time job, I thought, I can do this. . . . But I wasn't concerned about [repaying the loans], really. I was more envious of the kids who were qualified to borrow so much money that they didn't have to work!

Although his loans would eventually require a monthly payment of $355, more than double $160 per month, that amount of $160—what his friends were paying—stuck in his head. That was what he assumed his own loans would cost. He says of his first year in art school:

> I got into school, I got the loans, my parents were excited. They said, 'We'll pay your rent, just go to school, you can work a part-time job so you can have money for this and that.' That lasted for two months. And then my dad lost his job. . . . And that was where it all started to unravel. I mean, I don't blame them. But I thought, this is bulls**t. Now I have to pay everything. I have to pay the rent, I have to pay for school. And then I started to get really pissed off and thought, I don't want to go to school anymore, this is a waste of money.

Gray left school after two years and then returned after a few years and a period of unemployment. He attended classes for another year and a half, but was unable to graduate due to nonpayment.

He managed to avoid his loans for a few years. He nearly forgot about them; he pushed them into the corner of his mind where he could pretend they didn't exist. As far as he was concerned, he shouldn't have to repay loans for something that he never received (a BA). But one day, of course, his loans finally caught up with him. Gray walked into the office where he'd been working and discovered that his paycheck was nearly half of what it should have been. Confused and upset, he sought out the office manager, who informed him that she'd gotten a letter from the company overseeing his loans and that the missing loan payments had been taken from his wages automatically. He called the company in question, who demanded $700-a-month loan payments; Gray eventually negotiated it down to $355 per month.

That humiliating and humbling moment, standing there with half a paycheck, was when Gray says that he finally realized he would actually have to repay his loans. Before that, his loans had been an abstract concept, something he tried not to think about. But when his student loans interfered with his job, Gray came back to earth. "It was like an anvil hitting me on the head. When I got that paycheck from my work, with half of it gone, and that was how I found out—and my work was so unsympathetic. . . . Welcome to reality. Really fast."

Perhaps $66,000 might not sound like a lot of debt to you, but for someone like Gray, whose only goal is to become a successful working artist, it's become a nearly impossible amount of money to repay. Many artists work day jobs, but literally only to pay their rent, utilities, and materials; the fewer hours they can work, the better. Working more only increases the amount of time they *don't* spend doing what they love and are trained to do, be it painting, drawing, or sculpting. Many artists will tell you, as well, that their graduate programs were where they really grew as artists, and began to find commercial success. For someone like Gray, not only does his lack of a BA make graduate school nearly impossible, but he literally could not afford to go. Although Gray's situation is severe, his advice to young artists is certainly something worth thinking about:

I would tell some 18 year old, who maybe thought he was an art star in high school, to just go to a four-year, *affordable* university. If you want to be an artist, go to graduate school. That's where galleries pull from. They don't care about undergraduates. . . . No one will pay attention to undergraduates. Don't do your undergrad at art school. . . . If you're going to go into art, then always look at the most affordable ways to learn. It's usually through your friends. Just create a crew of other artists that you can pull from.

If you can't relate to Gray—if you read his story and think, "I will never be like that; I will choose a lucrative major and career, graduate, and be able to pay back my student loans no matter what the cost"—we've got news for you.

If you can get a job right after you graduate, the best jobs can often be the lowest-paying ones—internships or low-level positions that allow you to acquire the connections and networks you'll need to move ahead in your career during later years. But if you've got an $800 monthly loan payment to repay, you *will not be able* to take an unpaid or minimum-wage internship at the Council on Foreign Relations or at *Vogue*—you'll have to take a higher-paying job, likely something *really boring*, just to make your monthly payments.

What does taking on a loan really mean?

When you take on a loan, you have to take on a promissory note that functions like any other legal contract: You agree to a set of terms. Those terms, according to the U.S. Department of Education, include the following (emphasis ours):

- Loan is to be used only for educational expenses.
- *Must be repaid including any fees and interest.*
- Must repay even if you do not complete your education.
- *Must repay within 10 years* unless they are consolidated or select special repayment options.
- Federal loans can be prepaid without penalty.

- Minimum monthly payment will be at least $50.
- *Repayment will begin six months after leaving school* or dropping to less than half time.
- If I fail to repay a loan, I may be considered in default, and the following may result:
  - *My default status may be reported to a national credit bureau and have a negative effect on my credit rating for seven years.*
  - The entire unpaid amount of my loan, including interest, may become due and payable immediately.
  - I may lose deferment and repayment options.
  - *My federal and state income-tax refunds and other federal payments may be withheld.*
  - *My wages may be garnished.*
  - I may be assessed collection costs, including attorney's fees.
  - I may be ineligible to receive any further federal or state financial aid.
  - I may be *ineligible to obtain a state professional license in my field.*
  - I may be *sued.*

Those terms are serious. When you take out a student loan, you absolutely must repay it. And as we described previously in this chapter, they're incredibly difficult to discharge or get rid of.

If you can't repay your student loans, you'll find it very, very difficult to achieve your dreams, like Gray. And although you might not be an artist, you'll have something that drives you. What is it? Are you passionate about good nutrition for children? Are you an advocate for women's rights? Do you love being outside and active every day? Are you committed to activities at your church, temple, mosque, or other religious or community institution? Are you a political animal who wants to be in the thick of the local, state, or federal government?

Those questions could determine who you become, but if you can't repay your loans, the only question you'll be asking yourself is: "How do I make enough money, and live cheaply enough, to pay off my loans?" Money, and the pursuit and redistribution of it, could become your only passion.

Although you might not see it, Gray is an excellent example of someone you *could be*: a person who knew who he was, what he wanted to do, but never sat down and did the simple math of what he was borrowing versus how much he might make. You could be the most ambitious, directed, and passionate student of all time, but if you don't do the math, you might borrow more than you can afford and wind up living in a tenement under an assumed name like Gray. We're serious! It can happen to anyone. So to really understand student loans, that's the first thing we're going to ask you to do: Learn about the math.

Money, money, money. . .

How much money do you think you'll make when you graduate?

Go ahead. Write it down.

Well, because writing a book is sort of a one-way street, we have no idea what that number looks like. But we *can* bet that the number you wrote down is based on previous conversations you've had with other people, sort of like how Gray's assumption of his student loan payments—$160—came from what he knew his friends were paying (and had nothing to do with his own situation). So let's try and figure out an income for you that is all about *you* and not about what you've heard from other people.

Open your computer's browser and head to PayScale.com, a website that tracks compensation data. You'll be able to enter all types of information—education, location, what kind of job at what kind of company—without giving out your personal contact information (scroll to the bottom of the page and skip any personal fields) and click on the offer for your profile. When you finish, the calculator should give you an estimated salary.

We decided to research a couple of options. For example, according to PayScale's calculator, a graduate with a BA in accounting from Augsburg College in Minneapolis who moves to Chicago and gets a job as a CPA for an insurance company will earn an average starting salary of $49,286. Does that sound like a lot of money to you? It's less than you think (although it's still pretty good). Let's break it down.

What does $49,286 get you in Chicago?

Each month you'll make about $4,107. Congratulations, you've achieved the 25 percent tax bracket! If you're single, claiming yourself you will receive $6,300 in deductions. You'll lose roughly $459 in federal income taxes, $314 in Social Security, $60 in Medicare, and $147 to the great state of Illinois (use smartasset .com to estimate state taxes). This leaves you with about $3,127 per month; subtract another $200 for health insurance (and hey, that's if you can get it cheap through your employer) and you're down to $2,927 and you haven't contributed to your 401K yet. But you don't live in a box on the street; you'll need an apartment. According to apartments.com, you can rent an unfurnished studio apartment in Lincoln Park (an upscale neighborhood in the city full of recent college grads) for about $1,000 per month; throw in your utilities (cell phone, electricity, internet, and gas) at around $400, transportation at $200 (that's for the subway and the occasionally late-night cab ride—forget about buying a car just yet), and your monthly income is down to $1,372 per month, or $343 per week—from a paycheck that you estimated at nearly $4,107 per month. And that's if you're a CPA—a relatively high-paying job, and a good fit for someone who majored in math. Throw in a student loan of $32,000 on a 10-year repayment term, and that monthly loan payment of $320.00 brings your disposable income down to just $251 per week for food, clothing, travel, and entertainment. Let's be real: You're not going to sit home and be a hermit. There are concerts to attend, movies, weddings, and parties to go to. That's fairly manageable for a CPA who lives in Chicago on about $36 per day; to someone who works in the arts (or someone like Gray, who barely works at all), that's a king's ransom.

If you've never heard of Augsburg, the college we used for this example, it's a mid-selectivity private liberal arts college in Minneapolis. Their 2015–2016 sticker price for tuition and fees is $35,465, but their average net price (the price that most students pay) is just $25,760, and the average grant received by students is $20,722. Their average annual student loan is $9,865. Augsburg is also Ruth's alma mater.

Other kinds of majors—say, anyone in the humanities—might not be so lucky as our CPA. Let's look at another young friend of ours. Red graduated from an elite college with a bachelor's degree in history. During college, she worked at one of the school's museums as a security guard, making minimum wage. She got her first job at a major art museum, in the education department. Her income that year was just $21,000—and it was remarkable that she was paid at all, considering the legions of unpaid interns (some of whom had more education—masters and PhDs—than she did) that worked for and with her. But, it was a fantastic job that allowed her to meet dozens of helpful, fascinating people and sit around all day looking at, and learning about, art. If that sounds like something you'd be interested in, read on.

What does $21,000 get you in New York?

Our young friend Red lived in New York City—but not on the fashionable, expensive island of Manhattan (or even in uber-hip Brooklyn). She lived in Astoria, Queens (just across the bridge from Manhattan and her office), and split a tiny one-bedroom apartment with her boyfriend. In NYC, housing is often the largest expenditure for young professionals (or indeed, anyone); her frugality and willingness to share her space brought her rent down to just $500 a month. After taxes, her monthly income was about $1,400; subtract that $500 rent and she was down to $900. Subtract a monthly $100 MetroCard for the subway (forget about cabs—no matter how high her heels were, she hoofed it), another $100 for utilities (shared with the aforementioned boyfriend), and she had just $700 with which to feed and clothe herself—about $175 per week, or $25 per day. Subtract a student loan payment of $320 ($32,000 in total debt, or $8,000 per year) and that $750 a month gets cut in (more than) half: $314 per month, or $78 per week (or $11 per day) to feed, clothe, and entertain herself. How did she do it? Well, she ate a lot of rice, and went to a *lot* of dinner parties, bringing handmade origami instead of a bottle of wine. She only saw movies in the park (where they were free). She didn't have health insurance that year, but luckily, she didn't break anything or get the flu, and her local Planned Parenthood took care of her birth control and annual OB/GYN visit. She rode her bicycle when she wasn't taking the subway, and she shopped in friends' closets (that is, borrowing) and at thrift stores. It was a brutal year, but the job was so amazing that she wouldn't have done it any other way. The punch that low-paying (but prestigious) arts job packed on her resume (Education Department, Major Art Museum) continues to help her to this day. It even factored into her admission into an Ivy League graduate school program. If her student loans had surpassed $32,000, there is *no way* she would have been able to take that important first job—and though she didn't live like a queen (or even like a middle-class person), it was worth it.

Not all humanities jobs lead to a life of dignified poverty. Let's think about other humanities jobs in other cities. If you'd like to be a writer, Los Angeles is a great place to get your start. There are hundreds of movies being made each year. Someday, you could make a lucrative back-end deal and become the next Oscar-winning billionaire screenwriter—or you could get a salaried studio job and do (pretty) well for yourself. According to PayScale, a recent UCLA graduate with a major in Creative Writing who gets a job as a script writer in Los Angeles could make $37,596 per year, on average.

What does $38,000 get you in Los Angeles?

After taxes (which are high in California), your $37,596 goes down to about $30,070. That's $2,506 per month. According to apartments .com, a two-bedroom apartment to share in Los Feliz (a hip, amenity-rich neighborhood filled with young creative professionals) could cost an average of $1,000 per person, per month. Subtract that $1,000, and you're down to $1,506; take away another $200 for utilities (you'll need less electricity for heating and cooling in that perfect 75-degree L.A. weather) and you're down to $1,306. It's L.A., so you'll need a car. No subways for you. If you'd like to buy a new car, you can purchase a new Ford Fusion with a 72-month payment at 1.9 percent for $286 per month; that leaves you with $1,020 per month, or $255 per week. Take away $35 per week for gas, another $20 per week for car insurance, and you're down to $200 per week, or about $29 per day, with which to feed, clothe, and entertain yourself—and pay your student loans or health insurance. What are you going to do? Well, we think you should move. If you can share a three-bedroom apartment in Little Armenia, the next neighborhood over, with more friends, your rent could come down to just $600 per month and your utilities down to $100 (more people use more electricity, and want things— especially in L.A.—like cable TV or a cleaning service). That gives you an extra $500 per month, easily enough to cover your $320 student loan payment. You can put the remaining $100 away for health insurance. We would also suggest you buy a good, used car with a limited warranty. That will cost you another $200 per month and get you where you're going!

If science is what interests you, you're in luck. The United States has a multi-trillion-dollar science economy, making everything from rockets and bombs to Viagra and solar panels. You're on the road to long hours in the lab and big payoffs at the bank. Let's pretend your favorite subject is chemistry, and for good measure, you're a southerner. According to PayScale, if you're a recent graduate of Berry College in Georgia who majored in biomedical

engineering, you could make an average of $54,529 as a biomedi-
cal engineer working for a pharmaceutical company. Where would
you go? If you're a good southern girl or boy, you'll head to Atlanta,
the nearest big city. It's got a great music scene, tons of nightlife,
and more importantly, a large professional economy.

What does $54,529 get you in Atlanta?

Hotlanta is *hot*. If you're a southerner, you'll know that you can't
live without central air-conditioning; if you're a Yankee, you'll
know you need it as soon as you step off the plane. According
to apartments.com, a one-bedroom apartment with central air
could run you an average of $900 per month in East Atlanta, a
young, walkable, and bohemian neighborhood. After taxes, your
monthly take-home pay is $3,396; subtract your rent of $900, utilities at $200 (your A/C could run for six to eight months of the
year), and a car payment of $271 per month and weekly over-
head of $55 for insurance and gas, and you've got $1,970 left
over to spend. Looks like you can afford health insurance ($200
per month) and a student loan of $32,000 ($320 per month) with
cash to spare, leaving you with $1,462 monthly, or $365 per week
for food, clothing, travel, and anything else you can dream up.
You won't be taking a private plane anytime soon, but you'll be
comfortable.

———

Unless you plan on a career in computer science, engineering, or complex mathematics, the range of $21,000 to $55,000 is a
reasonable, likely salary range for your first job after graduation.
Your first job is what can make or break your career—or even help
you figure out what you *never* want to do for money.

Another young friend of ours, who we'll call Kelly, studied
international relations at an elite university. After graduation,
he thought that law school—and its end result of a cushy, high-
paying job at a law firm—would be his ticket to happiness. His

first year out of undergrad was spent toiling away at a prestigious law firm—and counting the seconds, every day, until he could leave the office. The practice of law can be lucrative, but there's a cost. It can be boring, the hours are murder, and new lawyers can take decades to break into the real profit-sharing model of a firm: partnership. Kelly was unimpressed—in fact, *de*pressed—by the life he had assumed he wanted. After a year, Kelly—who had *always* been concerned first and foremost about his financial future—decided to take a chance. He left the law firm and started a new path as a PhD student in the humanities. Financial security is still important to him, he says, but he's discovered that emotional and intellectual security, the kind that only a job you really love can provide, has trumped the notion that money buys happiness. Thankfully, Kelly's low undergraduate debt (around $25,000 total) meant that he didn't have to worry about large repayment sums or interest tallying up during his seven years of graduate school. If Kelly had taken on any more student loans, he says, he would have had to stay in the law firm where he got his start, ticking away the hours, years, and then decades on the clock before he felt free enough to pursue what he really wanted. He would have lost the first half of his life to his student loans.

How many loans to take: the $8K Debt Challenge

In all of our previous examples, you may have noticed that we used the exact same student loan payment for each theoretical graduate in each city. That's not because all student loans are the same, but because that is the absolute most—the worst-case scenario of student loans—that you should expect to take out. A $320-per-month payment is normal for a federal student loan of $8,000 per year on a 10-year term, or $32,000 total. That amount is the absolute *most* you should spend on student loans. Ideally, you wouldn't borrow anywhere close to that much, but the federal limits will allow you to. Why do we suggest a cap of $32,000? Well, we've got two great reasons.

#1: Borrowing from the federal government is your best (and cheapest) bet

A total of $32,000 will keep you in loans that come directly from the federal government. The most money you can take out in federal loans is $31,000: freshmen, $5,500; sophomores, $6,500; and juniors and seniors, $7,500. That's a total of $27,000 in Direct loans for four years, and you're given an additional $4,000 in eligibility for summer tuition and other living expenses, should you require it or if it takes you more than four years to graduate. If your parents are not eligible for a PLUS Loan, your Direct loan eligibility skyrockets—but that doesn't mean you should take any more than we recommend. Your loans will be a mix of subsidized and unsubsidized loans. Subsidized loans have less interest than unsubsidized; for a sub loan, the government does not charge interest while you're still in school. We're giving you $1,000 for either a Perkins Loan or credit card debt; that's enough to cover occasional incidentals, like travel costs for extracurricular activities, the loss of part-time income from taking an unpaid internship for one semester, or traveling while studying abroad. With $8,000 per year in loans, and income from a part-time job during the summer or on weekends, there's no need to take out any private loans (the kind with high interest that come from a private bank), ever. *Federal loans are the absolute best kind of loans you can take, for the following reasons*:

- With federal loans, interest rates are set. They don't change with LIBOR rates or adjust with the prime. That means that from the very beginning, you'll know exactly how much debt you're taking on. Remember: Student loan debt isn't just the amount you borrow; it's also the interest you pay for borrowing the money. Federal student loans of $32,000 require repayment of at least an additional $12,190.70, bringing your total debt to $44,190.70 or more.
- You don't need a cosigner with a federal loan. This is very important; a cosigner is someone who agrees

to repay your loans if you cannot do so. They take on the same responsibility for the loan that you do. If you don't pay, your cosigner has to. And that "has to" is an absolute.

- You don't choose your payment program when you take out the loan. With most private student loans, you have to select the repayment terms when you take out the loan, and what might look "doable" during your freshman year of college may be completely unmanageable when you graduate. But then, you'll be stuck. If you don't pay your loans, your wages could be garnished and you could be sued.

#2: Total student loan debt-to-income ratio should be 15 to 18 percent of your first-year income

Most financial planners have different approaches to finances, but they all agree on one thing: Your total student loan payment should be *less than or equal to* 15 to 18 percent of your annual income your first year out of college. That means if you're going to major in the liberal arts—whose 2015 graduates have an average starting salary of $39,931—your total debt cannot be more than $39,931. From a monthly, not annual, perspective, this means that your monthly student loan payments should not exceed 15 to 18 percent of your monthly gross.

There are financial planners out there who suggest that if you go to an elite or Ivy League college, you can safely take on more debt. We are not those kinds of advisors. *We cannot find any statistical evidence anywhere that suggests taking on more debt for college is an intelligent thing to do.* Your undergraduate, or bachelor's degree, *is not the same thing as a law or medical degree.* It does not "pay back" in the same way that people think law school and med school does; an undergraduate degree is the new high school diploma. It's an essential—not a bargaining foothold in the payroll office. Almost everyone you will ever work with in a professional environment (particularly a corporate one) will have gone to college. It's standard. Going to college, despite the oft-quoted statistic that "a college degree is worth an extra million dollars over one's lifetime," is not very lucrative anymore. Saying that is a completely dated idea that will not be true for your generation (unless inflation spikes and a million bucks is what you use to buy a loaf of bread, like in Zimbabwe). It's the equivalent of saying, "The Ford Model-T is the best car on the market!" Clearly, the Model-T is no longer the "best" car on the market; there are better cars (and better graduate degrees and resumes) out there. Don't be fooled by financial advisors who haven't realized what decade they live in. Spend as little as you can on the best education possible. Brand name will only be important insofar as a brand name *identifies* a community; how that community rallies around its members changes from school to school and has *absolutely nothing* to do with the ratings imposed on them by publications like the *Princeton Review* and *U.S. News & World Report*.

Meeting the $8K Debt Challenge

We challenge you, students and parents, to meet our $8K Debt Challenge. Don't take on a dime more than $8,000 per year, or $32,000 total, in loans. If the schools you're looking at will cost too much, *don't go there.* Find a different school, one that will value who you are as a student and give you a scholarship. Believe us, $32,000 in loans—which means $32,000 more than you're *already paying out of pocket*—is enough for your college education. Spend any more and you begin to slide uncontrollably down the slippery slope of debt. In the previous screenwriter scenario, this debt level represents 15 percent of take-home pay. That's in the acceptable range. But, when you add in a car payment and some credit card debt, it creeps close to the "distress" level of 40 percent. *If you can't meet our challenge, your student loan payments will outweigh the benefits of your college education.*

To estimate whether you can meet our $8K Debt Challenge, turn to Chapter 7 and use our Cost-Conscious Search chart at the end of the chapter. Once you've applied, been accepted, and received your final aid awards, use the three-step process we outline in Chapter 10.

The dangers of credit cards

On the flip side, if you don't take on enough debt to support yourself while you're in college (and income from a part-time job isn't enough), you'll be tempted to head down the yellow brick road of credit cards. We know that *everyone* warns you against the dangers of credit cards, and there's a reason for that. They're dangerous, and really—there's no good reason for you to have one. An "emergency" credit card quickly turns into a "just this once" repository for iTunes purchases, impulsive online shopping, trips to the bar, and so on. The deferred payments can really mess with your head, and before you know it, you wind up with a mountain of credit.

If you come from an affluent family or community and you're used to having nice things whenever you'd like them, the shock of being what we call "college broke"—the genteel poverty of most college students who live on ramen, dining hall food, and PBR—can send you tumbling down the rabbit hole into a bad credit trip that can last for years or even decades.

Clay came from an affluent community in which at least 90 percent of his peers went on to a four-year university; he describes his college experience as "an extension of high school." He says he grew up "never knowing the value of a dollar . . . I was always in a bubble, and being taken care of. Nothing bad ever happened to me." He had credit cards from the age of 15 onward. Clay always assumed his parents could pay for whatever debt he accrued, but their divorce and other financial difficulties prevented them from doing so. During college, Clay took out loans, worked multiple jobs, and racked up credit card debts to support his financially reckless lifestyle, which included, he says, things like weekend plane trips to major cities "just to go to Abercrombie & Fitch." His mother has tried to help him pay off his credit card and student loan debts, which currently total around $85,000. In order to help him, she's extended the entire line of home equity credit on her home, and now owes the bank more than she paid for their family house 25 years ago. She has also taken a second job, just to pay his debts. Clay says:

> I'm ashamed of what I've actually done to my family . . .
> I'm not saying the onus isn't completely on me—but a lot
> of it was my upbringing. My parents did not structure my
> behavior and teach me the value of a dollar. And I'm so
> thankful for my mom, for coming in and bailing me out—
> but she's done it now five times. When is enough *enough*?
> And we're at a point now—my mom shares her finances
> 100 percent with me—you know, *there is no more money*.
> We just went through all of the credit cards . . . I owe my
> mom more than what she's given me. And it sucks.

He's currently repaying his mother with a $500 payment each month; he estimates that he owes her roughly $45,000 dollars. The strain on his family, and his personal relationship with his mother, is actually *worse* than owing money:

> I'm 30, living on the other side of the country from my
> mom, and I haven't talked to her in a couple of weeks, and
> she can't tell me what to do—but I owe her all this money.
> And that has an impact on our relationship, and it's that
> hold when I go home. It's in every conversation, that I owe
> her money. And that sucks.

Clay's story is particularly unsettling because of the nature of his purchases: clothes, restaurants, bars, and travel. He didn't purchase a home he couldn't afford, or an exotic pet. His everyday purchases eventually became a landslide, and then an avalanche, of debt. His debt, and his understanding of what it meant to buy something on credit, didn't catch up with him until the last few years.

How could that happen, you might think? Well, we cover this in more depth in Chapter 4, but money—and the debts we owe when we spend money we don't have—is easy to hide from ourselves. We push it into the furthest recesses of our minds; unlike other problems, like alcoholism or drug addiction, credit-card debt is invisible. Other people can't see it, and it's generally considered impolite and embarrassing to talk about. The only person who can really wake you up to your debt is you—and a collection agency.

Clay is a soft-spoken person who speaks generously of his family and takes absolute and total responsibility for his debt. His willingness to talk to us, and to open up his heart to us and to you, demonstrates his deep understanding of the situation he's found himself in—but it may be too little, too late.

Parents, be aware: Stories like Clay's are not created in a vacuum. Often, credit habits are modeled after our parent's spending patterns. He says of his upbringing:

> When I was that young, I was way too strong-willed. The world was my oyster, and I just wanted to go explore, and I wasn't smart at all. I wasn't taught [about finances]. When you're getting $2,000 worth of presents at Christmas parties every year, and then next year your parents say, "It's kind of been a rough year—so here's only $1,500 worth of stuff," it's kind of like, "What the [heck]? Now you're going to send me off into the world, and I need to figure out [money] for myself?" It doesn't work. I would never blame my mom, but there's no reason I should be in this situation. I never had my mom sit down and do a basic budget with me—as far as how much are you making, what's your intake, what's your outtake. Nobody ever did that with me. I had to do it on my own. And I'm still learning.

Understanding borrowing capacity

We have many friends who went to graduate school, including Ruth herself and Carol's husband. Graduate school is wonderful; we've heard it described as being "back in an intellectual comfort zone rivaled only by the womb." You can hone your professional skills or spend a decade immersed in research on a specific thing; it's how you become a doctor, a lawyer, or a scientific expert. There are very few experiences that can rival the feeling of being in a room full of brilliant people, whose minds merge as they explore new boundaries of thought and interpretation. It's infectious and it's exhilarating. Unlike college or high school, you're not still "learning" in the same arduous way; your mind moves into fifth gear, along with a group of your peers. Graduate school is not only a wonderful way to grow your mind and advance your career, but also a place where you can make lifelong friends.

Graduate school is often used to increase your standard of living—to get you that promotion you've been eyeing, to change careers, or otherwise push your life forward: become a doctor or a nurse, or a full professor instead of an adjunct instructor. And that's all well and good; we clearly like and value education. But the price of many graduate programs is significantly higher than undergraduate, with places like Stanford's Graduate School of Business estimating a whopping $179,390 in total cost of attendance for the 2016–2017 year for their MSx program. If you're married and have two children, Stanford estimates you'll need more than $242,602 dollars just to make it through a year (including rent and groceries). And although that may be the highest graduate cost of attendance we've ever come across, graduate school is still generally more expensive than undergraduate— about $30,000 or more, per year. On average, the annual net price of tuition for a four-year public undergraduate education is $18,110; for a master's degree at a public school, it's $20,850. At private colleges, where an undergraduate education has an average annual net price of $36,589, a master's degree will cost, on average, $44,340 for tuition each year.[1] Why so high? Well, employers often subsidize, or help pay for graduate degrees for their employees, which drives up the price for people who are looking to change careers. In the case of professional degrees such as medicine or law, the de facto assumption that graduates will make enough money to repay their degrees (and indeed, often view either profession as a guaranteed gravy train) means that the market value of the degree—that is, what they can get away with charging—is very high.

Some graduate programs will fund you (give you tuition and living expenses) while you study. But the rest will be primarily on your own dime. Let's look at the total costs of two popular, usually unfunded, pay-out-of-pocket graduate degrees.

Medicine

Ouch! Excuse the pun, but it's painfully expensive to become a doctor. The Association of American Medical Colleges says that the average student loan debt of med school graduates is $172,751. Depending on the repayment method you choose (and assuming it's all in federal loans—you can take out larger loans when you're a grad student), that's a monthly loan payment anywhere from $1,400 to $1,800 *per month*. A $2,200 monthly student loan bill will have an enormous influence over what kind of medicine you practice, where you live, when you can buy a home of your own, save for your children's college, and even your own retirement. So if you're thinking about med school down the line, it might be a good idea to go right out of college. You might burn out, but at least you could be done with your student loan payments by the time you're ready to buy a house.

Law

If you'd like to become a passionate defender of the underprivileged, make sure you choose a law school that discounts for public-interest law. Otherwise, your student loan debt from law school will average $84,000 if you go to a public school and $122,158 if you go to a private. So following the 1:1 ratio, our debt rule of thumb that parallels the 15 to 18 percent advice from financial planners, you'll need to make at least $84,000 your first year out of law school. Luckily, the average salary for law graduates is $60,000. That's around $800 per month in student loans—a big chunk out of a monthly salary of $5,000.

If you're already carrying debt from undergrad, adding the cost of graduate school to your total debt will be onerous, to say the least. It might be worth it, but you should keep further borrowing (also known as your borrowing capacity) in mind when you're looking at colleges. The more you borrow now, the less you may be able to borrow later—and the higher your debt goes, the more significantly it affects your life.

The final word on borrowing

This is our rule: Don't take out a dime more than $32,000 total, or $8,000 per year. That's already a lot of money; we sincerely hope that you'll think twice about borrowing even *half* of that. So for the risk-averse among you, we'll be more strict: Don't take out a dime more than $16,000 total, or $4,000 per year—any more than that and you'll be worried about it until you're 30.

Student loans are not free, not something to discard; they are a real and serious obligation that, if unmet, could ruin a decade of your life or more. Don't be disabled by the cost of your education. Borrowing is supposed to help you, not hurt you.

A life indentured to enormous student loan payments means that at *best*, you'll spend your 20s bored out of your mind at a bill-paying snoozefest. At worst, you'll be living under an assumed name, working cash-only jobs, and running from bill collectors. So become instead the educated person who seizes *all* the joy, adventure, and success—however you might define it—that you can out of your life. Don't borrow a dime more than $32,000 to go to college.

You, Your Parents, and Their Money

WELCOME TO THE most uncomfortable part of the book!

As far as conversational topics go, money is *awful*. It's unpleasant and frequently leads to conflict. Chances are, you, or your parents, or all of you together, have been putting off this discussion. You probably don't know very much about your parents' financial situation, other than that you need financial aid to go to college. Most people don't share their finances with their children, so you're not alone.

The goal of this chapter is for you to have a productive and helpful conversation about your parents' finances, and to figure out how your family is going to make your expected family contribution, or EFC. (If you're not familiar with the EFC, turn to Chapter 2.) But to do that, it's helpful to have an understanding of what "making money" might mean to your parents, of why it's hard for them to talk about, and why they might not have enough to give you.

Talking about money is weird and awkward for everyone, even for us—and we write about and think about money all the time. It's a strange thing. You'd think that because we live in

97

a capitalist economy—a winner-take-all wonderland that is so nakedly obsessed with dollars, greenbacks, dough, bucks, and bread—we would have a better relational vocabulary for talking about cash. But we don't. Money is a heavily loaded topic. Conversations about money, particularly with your children, skirt the edges of ego, of fear, of satisfaction, of success, of identity.

With a little bit of empathy and understanding, you can navigate this conversation with ease. It's best to start off with FAFSA4caster and estimate your EFC before you talk about whether or not your parents can meet it. You can do this your freshman, sophomore, or junior year of high school. You can even do it in middle school! It's *never* too early to start talking about money (but it will always be a little awkward).

Before you have "the money talk" with your parents, please ask them to read Chapter 2 and Chapter 5, which is written specifically for parents. It won't take them more than an hour, and it'll give everyone a good understanding of all the terms and phrases you'll need in the coming months and years. It's an easy thing to ask— just put a sticky note on top of the book with the words, "Please read Chapters 2 and 5."

Step 1: Predict your EFC with FAFSA4caster

Ask your parents to sit down and talk with you about paying for college—the first of what will probably be several conversations. You'll need a computer with a working internet connection to use FAFSA4caster (don't use your phone, use a real computer because there are several fields to fill out), and a blank sheet of paper with a pen.

When is a good time to get your parents' attention? Certainly not over the breakfast table, or at the end of a long workday. We suggest asking your parents two to three days in advance if they can set aside some time to talk to you about paying for college; you'll need an hour or so. Say the following words:

Mom and Dad (or "Mom and Mom," "Dad and Dad," "Betty and Dad," "Mom and Charlie," or just "Mom" or "Dad"), would it be possible for you to set aside some time to talk to me on (insert day here) about how we're going to pay for college? I've been reading about financial aid, and I think we should talk about it. I need your help. What's a good time for you?

The most important thing is to *be polite*. As the German philosopher Arthur Schopenhauer so famously expressed, "Politeness is to human nature what warmth is to wax." Speak evenly and reasonably; if your parents won't respond favorably, just repeat, over and over, that you *need their help*. And keep asking until they relent! Persistence is one of the great traits of successful people. You don't get what you want unless you *ask for it*. And sometimes, with people, you have to ask several times. That's just the way it goes. So don't get mad. Just get what you want. You'll wear them down eventually.

It might sound smarmy, but if you did have to ask your parents several times to have this conversation with you, start by saying *thank you*. Be genuine! Thank them for their willingness to talk with you about college; for the things and opportunities they've provided for you, and their willingness to help you invest in your future. Although it's always a choice to have children, parents sincerely appreciate being thanked for all that they've done. Expressing your gratitude (as soon as you start saying thank you, you'll find that you really do mean it) is a wonderful way to warm up the conversation and get everyone on the same page. If you need to, make a list of all the things you're thankful for.

If your parents are married to each other, talk to them together; if they're divorced, talk to them separately. If they are divorced, it's a good idea to speak with the parent who claims you as a dependent *first*; that's the parent whose financial information will be on the FAFSA. *Helpful hint:* If your parents are divorced, always file with the parent who has a smaller annual household income—household, not individual. This is assuming they live in the same city and state, and that you could reside with either parent. For some students, that's not the case; one of your parents has moved out of state, gone to Bali to eat/pray/love, or doesn't have a stable environment for you. In that case, don't worry about it. But if you can file as a dependent of a parent who makes less money, do so. That will give you a lower EFC than if you file with the wealthier parent, and you can use the FAFSA4caster to figure out what the difference would be.

Anyway, you'll ask your parents a few days in advance for their time, and then hopefully you'll sit down together at the kitchen table with a computer, a blank sheet of paper, and a pen or pencil. Turn off your cell phone (and theirs!). Your parents might ask you what kind of college you plan on going to, and how much you think it's going to cost. Frankly, it doesn't matter—wherever you go to college, your EFC will be the same, so you should find out what it is as soon as you can. Whether you go to a public or a private school, you're planning on making up the remainder of the costs through loans and aid. Show your parents the following formula:

Direct costs (tuition, room and board, and fees) – **EFC** (what you'll figure out today) = **The amount you need in aid, including scholarships and loans**

Your parents *don't* have to be responsible for this amount. If they can contribute to it, great; if not, you're going to try and get enough in financial aid to make it work. *If you're in the top 25 percent of applicants at most colleges, you've got a very good chance of getting the best need- and merit-based aid award available.*

That means, if your parents ask you what kind of college you plan on going to, the answer is: "A college where I'm in the top 25 percent of applicants, and I can get funded."

Say it with pride! This is *your* education. You're taking charge. But what does that mean for your parents? It simply means they have to figure out how to meet your EFC; you'll take care of the rest. *Your EFC will be the same, no matter where you go to school.*

And although FAFSA isn't perfect, your expected family contribution is generally a pretty good indication of how much money your family *could* spend on college, and colleges take it into account when they award your aid. The federal government absolutely assumes that the first responsibility for paying for your college education rests with your parents. There's no two ways around that, so turn to page 111 if your parents refuse to pay at all. And if your parents are willing to commit more than their calculated EFC, fantastic; if not, you're willing to do enough research to find a college that will fund you.

Filling out the FAFSA4caster takes about 30 minutes. You'll go online, to fafsa4caster.ed.gov, and your parents will input their financial information. The FAFSA4caster doesn't save your information, or share it with anyone. Your parents may tell you exactly what their financial situation is; they may not. The beauty of FAFSA4caster is that they can fill it out with you, and you don't have to look at their income and assets if they don't want you to. But you *will* learn what your family's EFC is. It's important for you to understand how much your family is expected to be able to pay for college, because you may have to make some changes as a family in order to afford it.

At the end of FAFSA4caster, you can choose to compare the average cost of a private education to the average cost of a public education, in or out of state. When you submit the 4caster, it'll give you a summary page; your EFC will be at the top of the page. It'll be anywhere from 0 to 999,999; this is the whole dollar amount that your family should be able to pay out of pocket. Ask your parents to write it down on a separate sheet of paper. This is the most useful part of the FAFSA, and the most germane one to this chapter.

Below the EFC is a chart that estimates the amount you could theoretically get in federal aid. It includes loans, and Pell if you're eligible. We're not thrilled with this part of the FAFSA4caster; it tends to allow families to make an assumption, based on the 4caster estimate, of what the aid and loans will be—and it never looks like enough. Remember: The FAFSA4caster aid estimate is *only federal*—it does not estimate what you might get in need- or merit-based aid from a specific college or university, or grants from your home state.

As you can see from your summary, FAFSA will subtract the grants and loans that you're likely eligible for from the average cost of tuition, and show you an estimated gap at the bottom of the page. Please bear in mind that the cost of tuition used by FAFSA is an average *sticker* price; it doesn't use data based on what families actually pay, just what colleges and universities report that they *charge*. For more information about sticker price and net price, see Chapter 7.

The FAFSA4caster may have awarded you $9,000 or more in loans (two Direct loans and a Perkins, if you're eligible). You *do not have* to take out these loans, and *you should not use them to meet your EFC*. The EFC is a family responsibility; student loans will be yours, and you'll use them to meet your need (direct costs – EFC = your need). We're not against loans; a reasonable amount of student loans can help build credit and responsible financial behaviors, and ultimately, you, the person who is receiving the education, should be responsible for paying as much as you can. But as we discussed in Chapter 3, student loans can easily become unreasonable—and unmanageable. Take out your sheet of paper, where you've already written down your EFC. Next to that, write down the amount in loans that FAFSA4caster predicts you'll be eligible for.

Step 2: Understand loan repayment with Finaid.org

Before you start talking with your parents about how your family can meet your EFC, it's important to cover the loan question that your FAFSA summary raised. *Remember: You won't be using your loans to meet the EFC. Meeting the EFC is your parents' responsibility.* FAFSA4caster gave you an estimate of how much you'll be eligible for in loans; your parents may assume that you will take out the maximum. So while you're sitting together in front of a computer, log on to finaid.org and navigate to their calculators. Multiply the loan amount you wrote down on your sheet of paper by 4 (for four years of college) and enter that number into the loan calculator. The calculator will give you the standard federal interest rate of 3.76 percent. Leave it there. Select a 10-year term with a minimum payment of $50. Hit enter.

On the next page, you'll see a summary of what your monthly student loan payment could be. Ask your parents if they think it's manageable. We don't think that anything beyond $32K total in loans, or roughly $320 per month in repayment, is manageable for most college graduates; your parents may think differently. So it's time to ask a few questions:

- Do your parents want you to take on loans to meet your remaining need?
- If you take on loans and can't repay them, would your parents be willing to help you?
- Would they give you half, or make your monthly payments until you find a job?
- Do they think you should take out less money in loans?
- What's a reasonable amount?

Discuss and try to come to a conclusion about a reasonable total loan burden for your college education. You haven't taken out the loans yet; this is just a discussion about budgeting and student loans that every family should have. Often, parents are more willing to assist their children with additional college costs (if they have the funds available) once they realize what kind of debt their child could eventually assume.

Remember: Taking out loans doesn't change your EFC. You can apply a portion of them to your EFC if you absolutely need to, but they'll likely be part of your aid package.

Step 3: Meet your EFC

The FAFSA is great at divining two things: families that absolutely cannot pay and families that have boatloads of money. But the middle class often falls into a grey area in which the EFC can look like an astronomical amount of money.

It's not as bad as you think, and you don't have to pay it all in one lump sum. Your family probably has the money somewhere—but you're going to have to change your spending habits. Most colleges allow parents to pay their EFC with a 10-payment plan that extends from June to April, or July to May. Divide the EFC by 10. Your parents will need to meet that amount each month for 10 months of the school year, each year that you are in college.

If the EFC doesn't shock your parent(s), and they think it's reasonable, ask them to multiply the EFC by 1.5. This means that an EFC of $15,000 would become $22,500; an EFC of $20,000 would become $30,000; an EFC of $35,000 would become $52,500; and so on. That extra $7-, $10-, or even $17,000 dollars could mean the difference between attending a school that will fund you, and a school that won't. If you've got your heart set on some highly competitive places (where you may not be in the top 25 percent of the class), you might need the extra funds to make up for the lack of a scholarship. Remember: The bottom half of the class pays for the top half of the class. And if you can't demonstrate serious financial need for an elite college, and you'd be in the bottom of their academic class, you won't get much of a discount.

However, your family is probably not looking at the EFC and thinking, "That's all?" So this is where you're going to get creative. In order to meet your EFC, you and your parents need to discuss the following things (this conversation is the same for both intact families and the custodial and non-custodial parent):

- Have they put aside any funds, perhaps in a 529 savings plan, for your education? If so, these funds should be applied to your EFC. If not, better late than never! Ask your parents how much they can start putting aside—starting tomorrow. Even $200 per week will be $10,400 at the end of the year; even $100 per week will make a big difference.
- Do they have any large purchases planned for the next few years, such as cars, vacations, home repair, or care for a relative? If so, ask your parents if you can help them in some way. Instead of replacing the entire roof, would it be possible for you to help one of your

parents replace the leakiest section during the summer? Could you provide childcare for your siblings more often, or commit to ferrying an older relative to necessary appointments every Saturday for the next year? Ask your parents if they're willing to put some of their savings toward your education instead, and *negotiate*. Have them make a list of all the large purchases they plan on making in the next few years, and run down the list, item by item, suggesting ways in which you could help or somehow allay the financial burden. If you have a car, volunteer to sell it or give it to another sibling, and take yourself off your parent's car insurance.

- Do you have any grandparents or great-aunts and uncles? If so, you're in luck. There's only so many bridge tallies and Cadillacs that they can buy; older relatives often love to do something *real* for their grandchildren, other than send new socks and checks for $27, and sometimes they have the portfolio to do so. Do your parents think they would be willing to contribute to your college education? If so, how much? Let your parents know that you don't need birthday or holiday gifts from your older relatives, and ask them what they'd prefer. Should they broach the subject with Grandma? Should you?

- If your grandparents are willing to help, the best way to go about it is for them to open up a 529 savings plan on your behalf, or use a Coverdell account or savings bonds. For more information on the 529 plans available in your state, go to our website at thefinancialaid handbook.com.

- If your grandparents went to college, look into legacy scholarships. Are you interested in going to the same school they did? If so, there may be a legacy scholarship available for you. To find out more, look on the college's website, or call the admission office directly (you can always find the phone number on the site, under "Contact Us") and ask if there are legacy scholarships available. If your grandparents (or parents) served in the military, you might also be eligible for veteran's scholarships. Go to the American Legion website, legion.org, and look through their online "Need a Lift?" booklet, which lists scholarships, tuition costs, and federal and state grants that could benefit direct descendants of veterans.

• Grandparents also often belong to some kind of fraternal organization, like the Elks, Moose, or an ethnic-based organization (the Polish Ladies' Auxiliary, etc.), the AARP, or a union. Often, those organizations have college scholarships for relatives or descendants of members. Ask your grandparents what organizations they belong to, and then contact their local chapters (or look on the website, if they have one) for scholarship information. It's not the most reliable route, but it's always a possibility and worth looking into.

Be prepared to list what you're able and willing to do, aside from taking out loans, to pay for your college education. Will you be working during the summer? If so, how many summers? Would you be willing to put a portion of your income from an after-school job toward your college education? Are you willing to babysit younger siblings, or take over chores that might be hired out (like cleaning, raking, mowing the lawn, dog-walking, or car-washing) from now until you start college? Make a list of everything you could do during your remaining years in high school and your summers home from college (discount the summer between your junior and senior year from college—you will likely need to take an unpaid internship) to help contribute to the EFC, if your parents need you to. Remember: It's always cheaper to save than it is to borrow (that is, it will ultimately cost you less to *earn* the money than it will to take it out in loans).

Remember: No matter where you go to college, your EFC will be the same. So before you even *visit* colleges, your family needs to make sure that you can find a way to meet your EFC.

Divorced and/or blended families

Divorce can shatter the best-laid schemes of mice, men, and college tuition. Unless parents have carefully spelled out who pays for what, college tuition can be the last thing on their minds. If your parents *do* have a written agreement, you'll have to ask them what it is, and then stick to it. If your parents need to re-negotiate the terms of their agreement (due to job loss or any other change in their financial circumstances), ask them to do that as soon as possible. But for the rest of you—those whose parents *don't* have written agreements about college tuition—you will have to have the same conversation twice. As a student, this sucks for you. We're sorry, but that's just the way it is: It's twice the amount of work. Fortunately, divorce—and everything that goes with it—is common enough that even the craziest-sounding situation will be old hat to your college's financial aid office, so for now, don't worry about explaining it down the line.

In terms of the EFC, you'll have to have the same conversation that you had with your custodial parent *again* with your non-custodial parent. Although the non-custodial parent's information may not be on the FAFSA, it takes two to tango. No one impregnates themselves: Both of your parents had a hand in creating you, so they are equally responsible for your college education, to the degree they are able. It's that simple.

The rule of thumb we like to go by for divorced parents is called *halfsies*. That's right: No matter whose financial information results in the EFC, your divorced parents should split it right down the middle. *If your divorced parents still live in the same city or town, and if you are able to live with the parent who makes the least amount of money for more than half the year, then that's the best financial decision you can make in terms of lowering your EFC.*

In that best-case scenario, regardless of whose income is responsible for determining your EFC, your parents should split the cost of the EFC in half. In terms of the FAFSA, the parent who is your legal custodian may not be your "custodial" parent; for the FAFSA, your custodial parent is simply the person you lived with the most (that is, more than half the year) during the last 12 months. How do you choose whose EFC to use? It's simple. The smartest thing to do would be to calculate the EFC of *each parent* separately, then bring both numbers to both sets of parents and ask them which EFC they would rather split: the higher EFC, or the lower EFC? If they're thinking straight, they'll want to split the lower EFC. Again, whichever parent has the lower EFC is the parent who you should consider your custodial parent, and the one you should live with for more than half of your senior year of high school (if you are able to). Splitting the lower EFC makes it reasonable for both parties. Now, there might be some griping about who makes more money or how they spend it or whose new wife or husband does what or whatever ridiculous thing they can think of. But the EFC is the responsibility of both parents; if they were still married, they would share it. Just because they got divorced does not absolve them from taking care of *you*. We've had countless phone calls from whiny, embittered divorced parents, claiming that the other parent is responsible for more. Look: Two people make a baby. Maybe if your parents were young enough to be born into the age of financially accessible reproductive technology, three people (your dad's sperm, your mom's egg, and a scientist), four people (sperm donor, egg donor, surrogate, and scientist), or an entire laboratory made their baby. But there are always two names on a birth certificate: the names of your legal parents. They are equally responsible for the cost of your college education; they should split the EFC right down the middle. If a wealthier parent is willing and able to contribute additional funds, great—but the other parent is not obligated to match that additional amount if he or she is not able to.

Now, we know that halfsies might not always be possible. Sometimes parents make wildly different incomes from one another. Sometimes, you simply cannot live with one of your parents due to location, financial circumstance, illness, or even prison. If one of your parents is insanely wealthy, he or she should probably be the one to pay for your college education. What's insanely wealthy? Let's call it more than $250,000 per year. That's a high enough income to put your EFC through the roof, and possibly make it difficult for the other parent to split the EFC down the middle. That's also an income bracket where you'll get very little need-based financial aid, and you probably don't need to be reading this book. But those parents know who they are. And if one of your parents is making so little money that he or she cannot afford to house you for more than half the year, and really cannot afford in any way to help you with college, then the burden will likely be on the shoulders of the parent who makes the most. It's an unfortunate reality, and you'll need to discuss all of this with the financially responsible parent.

What about my stepparent(s)?

If one or both of your parents have remarried, the income of their spouses—your stepparent(s)—will be considered in the FAFSA (the custodial parent's spouse) and/or the PROFILE (both households, custodial and non-custodial). Stepparents, however, often have their own financial responsibilities, like their own children (your step-siblings) or their own elderly relatives (step-grandparents and step-great-grandparents). If, when one or both of your parents remarried, they signed a pre-nuptial agreement that precludes the stepparent from paying for any of your college education, that agreement is void; the reason is that two parties cannot make an agreement that binds a third party (in this case, the third party is the federal government). Your custodial parent's spouse is required by law to include his or her assets in the FAFSA. If, however, the financial obligations of that stepparent include other college tuitions, that obligation will be included in the FAFSA the same way that any legal siblings (blood relatives or adopted siblings) would be. If those step-siblings consider your custodial stepparent to be *their* non-custodial parent, their information won't be included (but all alimony and paid child support will be).

Stepparents, both custodial and non-custodial, are tricky. They're not your actual parents, but they did marry into your family, and by law, took on all of your parent's family and financial obligations. They may not feel as though they should be responsible for your college tuition, but by law, their information is included in the FAFSA. We recommend that you include the custodial step-parent in all conversations about college tuition; the non-custodial step-parent *does not* have to be included.

You should also know that different schools have different expectations. If you've already got a list of your top schools, go online, and look up the phone number for the school's financial aid or admission office; it should be listed either under "Prospective Students," "Admission," or "Contact Us." We recommend that you call them, identify yourself as a prospective student, ask politely if the person on the end of the line has a moment to answer your questions, and then explain your situation as quickly and as thoroughly as you can. We do recommend that you call, because this kind of information is not usually communicated in financial aid brochures or on the college's website. So if you've got a list of schools going already, and you have a tricky divorce or blended family situation, we encourage you to contact your top-choice schools early and learn about their expectations.

If one or both of your parents are engaged, we recommend that they understand and discuss the financial ramifications of getting married while you're in college. For the soon-to-be stepparent, there are very few benefits to absorbing your family's financial responsibilities—and quite a few negatives, the largest being a legal responsibility for meeting your EFC each year until you graduate college. It's fairly simple to broach this topic with them: Just ask your soon-to-be step-parent how he or she feels about paying for your college education. If the answer is "That's not my responsibility," let them know that FAFSA disagrees and that their additional income will change your financial aid award for the worse. Then let them know that you love having them around—but that living together until you graduate might be the best possible financial decision for everyone.

What if my divorced parents don't speak to each other?

If your parents don't speak to each other, then you will need to assume a role that you're probably already quite familiar with: the role of the adult. Sometimes divorced people can be so childish that we cannot believe they manage to function in other areas of life. You're going to need to ask your parents a simple question: Which EFC would they rather pay half of? The higher EFC, or the lower EFC? Calculate the EFC of *each parent* with the FAFSA4caster, and then bring both numbers to your parents. They're going to have to split one; make them choose. If they have an ounce of sense, they'll choose the lower EFC. The parent with the lower EFC is the parent who should claim you as dependent, and the one you should consider the custodial parent.

What if my divorced parents are best friends?

Oh, you lucky duck. If your divorced parents are the best of pals, they can work this out between themselves. Have them each read the second half of this chapter, and ask them to make a plan! Have the three-step conversation we outlined earlier in this chapter with both of them at the same time.

Deadbeat dads and moms

Some students, and it might be you, have one parent who is a *total jerk*. These are known as Deadbeat Dads (DBDs) and Moms (DBMs). They mostly come into the equation when you're applying to a college that requires the CSS PROFILE, which requests documentation from both the custodial and non-custodial parent. The CSS PROFILE is administered by the College Board, a nonprofit organization that also administers AP testing and coursework. A list of schools that require the PROFILE can be found at bigfuture .collegeboard.org. If you're applying for early decision, most colleges will require the CSS PROFILE along with the FAFSA.

Deadbeat Dads and Moms like to punish their ex-spouse by denying *you*, their child, financial support. How this punishes the other parent, we're not quite sure. Mostly, it just punishes *you*, and often irreparably damages your relationship. Deadbeat Dads and Moms are people who operate with a limited set of logic and morals. They cannot see the forest for the trees; they cannot let their love of you, their child, dissolve their hatred for their former spouse. These parents know who they are. And we, as former admission and financial aid directors, know who they are too. That's the good news.

Every college and university that you will apply to has a protocol for Deadbeat Dads and Moms (also known as a "non-custodial parent who refuses responsibility for payment"). But in order for you to be able to work within this system, you've got to start documenting your DBD or DBM today. You will need to dry your tears, find your strength, and get a pen! Write down the time and date of each conversation you have with them about college payment, and write down what they said to the best of your recollection. You must document their refusal to support you or to fill out the PROFILE in order to get a waiver of non-custodial information. That will happen down the line, after you've already applied to colleges, but it helps to document their behavior as soon as you can. Just write it down in a notebook or in a Word doc on your computer with times and dates; if you can get other documentation, like unpaid child support, that's helpful too. Photocopy all official documents and keep them in a folder marked DBD or DBM. Note: DBD and DBM are not official financial aid terms. But sometimes it helps to call a deadbeat a deadbeat. Hopefully, you've got at least one decent parent, aunt, uncle, grandparent, or foster parent to take care of you, and you don't need a crazy deadbeat dad or mom interfering in your life. So let them be crazy; just *document* their craziness. It will help you in the long run, and you don't *really* need that person to move on with your life and go to college.

What if *both* parents refuse to pay or fill out the FAFSA?

Your parents must fill out the FAFSA if you want to get any financial aid. They may be laboring under the assumption that if they *don't* pay or fill out the FAFSA, you'll get *more* aid; that is absolutely *not true.* The federal government, which gives billions of dollars to colleges not only in federal student aid but in actual dollars, assumes that the responsibility to pay for college lies first with the family of the student. Turning 18 and moving out of the house doesn't change that; until you are 24 years of age or older, you're considered a dependent by the FAFSA. If your parents are the kind who think "good children pay for their own education," they should be aware that they will raise your college costs significantly, likely to the sticker price, if they do not fill out the FAFSA. *You won't be able to take out federal loans or qualify for any federal grants unless your parents fill out the FAFSA.*

The next chapter is written specifically for your parents; we recommend that they take a look at it before you sit down to discuss your EFC. And after you've taken these three steps (predicted your EFC, calculated your possible loan burden, and discussed ways you can help your parents meet the EFC) it's a great time to start looking at colleges. Go on to Chapter 6 and use our Merit Aid Profile, or MAP, to begin your strategic search for colleges at which you'll be in the top 25 percent of applicants.

For Parents: You, Your Children, and Your Money

THE GOAL OF this chapter is to help you and your spouse (if you have one) figure out how to predict and meet your expected family contribution (EFC). The EFC is a number, in actual dollars, that is calculated by the Free Application for Federal Student Aid (FAFSA). The FAFSA is used by all colleges and universities to determine your child's financial aid award. You and your child will need to fill out the FAFSA if you want to receive *any* need-based financial aid from your child's college of choice.

The FAFSA can be submitted as early as October 1 of the year prior to enrollment. For example, if your child is planning on attending college in the fall of 2018, that means you may submit the FAFSA on or after October 1, 2017, and you'll use your previous year's tax information from 2016. Even if you do not submit the FAFSA until the enrollment year, you will still use the tax information from the prior prior year (two years before the enrollment year).

Luckily, you can predict your EFC at any time by using the FAFSA4caster online at fafsa.ed.gov. It takes about 30 minutes to complete, and anything you input will not be forwarded to the federal government or individual colleges without your express permission. We love FAFSA4caster! It's a wonderful and extremely helpful tool, and it helps you determine what your EFC might be long before your child actually applies to and enrolls in college.

No matter where your child is planning on going to college—a community college, a large public, or a small private—your EFC will be the same. You will submit your basic financial information in the FAFSA, and the Department of Education will calculate, using a federal methodology, how much you could reasonably afford to spend on your child's college education. For more information about the FAFSA and how your EFC is calculated, turn to Chapter 2. We do recommend that you read all of Chapter 2 before reading any further into this chapter; it will give you a good understanding of all the terms and definitions you'll need to know.

After your child actually *applies* to colleges, the information from your FAFSA will be forwarded to the colleges (you'll have to stipulate which college(s) when you turn in your FAFSA, which you can do online). Each college will then calculate your child's remaining need (that is, scholarship dollars or tuition discounts they can receive) by using the following calculation:

Direct costs (tuition, room and board, and fees) – **EFC** (what you'll figure out today) = **The amount your child is eligible for in need-based aid, from both the federal government and the college itself**

If your child is in the top 25 percent of applicants (which you can determine by following our MAP process outlined in Chapter 6), they will have the best possible chance of getting the highest amount of need- and merit-based aid available. We recommend that students *only* apply to colleges at which they are in the top 25 percent of applicants; there are currently more than 4,400 colleges and universities in the United States, with varying degrees of competitiveness.

If you want your child to receive any need-based financial aid, you must fill out the FAFSA. All colleges and universities that accept federal financial aid dollars agree with the basic assumption that the primary responsibility for paying for a student's education rests with the family—not with the federal government; not with the college; not with the state government, but with the student and the family. You can't get around this. Simply declaring that you won't pay or refusing to fill out the FAFSA or PROFILE (another form that you may have to submit) will not change that obligation. For a list of colleges that require the PROFILE, go to bigfuture.org.

We understand that talking with your children about your finances is a thorny road. Most people don't do it; a pretty standard reason is that children cannot keep their mouths shut. If you tell them how much money you make, they'll tell the teller at the bank, the checkout girl at the grocery store, or their friends and teachers. Children, and especially teenagers, have absolutely no understanding of what it takes to make a living, and it's difficult to explain how much money you make. Children don't understand after-tax income, debt, assets, or financial obligations in the same way adults do. No matter what you say, your children may take one look at your new car or gadgets and may automatically assume that you have more discretionary or disposable income than you actually *do*. So we don't necessarily recommend telling your children exactly what your income is, and thankfully, with FAFSA and the FAFSA4caster, you don't have to; all you have to (and should) tell your children is what the FAFSA results in: your EFC.

In the previous chapter, we did our best to explain to your child how he or she should approach this conversation with you and why talking about money can be difficult for families. We've encouraged your child to initiate this conversation and to fully take responsibility for the pursuit of a college education. You might not be able to answer every question we've encouraged him or her to ask you, but we think it's important that your child has a general (*not* explicit) understanding of your household finances and obligations, and recognize his or her responsibility for the changes in household spending that you may have to make to meet your EFC.

We'll talk about the multiple ways you can meet your full EFC (and why you should) later in the chapter. For now, the most important thing is to actually calculate it with FAFSA4caster and get an idea of exactly how much money we're talking about.

Step 1: Predicting your EFC with FAFSA4caster

For intact families, this process is fairly simple: You and your spouse will sit down and calculate the EFC together. But for divorced or blended families, the EFC can be confusing. Whether you're the custodial or non-custodial parent you should calculate an EFC. (Regardless of who is the legal custodian in a divorce, FAFSA considers the custodial parent to be the parent with whom the child has lived with the most, that is, more than half the year, in the last 12 months.) We recommend that both parties fill out the FAFSA4caster and calculate an EFC because divorced parents who share custody often have trouble, unless there is a written agreement, deciding who pays for what. We think that (if you share custody and it is possible to have your child live with either parent for more than half the year) calculating both of your EFCs, then splitting the cost of the lower EFC, is the fairest way to settle this issue. And if your child is going to a school that requires the PROFILE, you'll *both* have to go through the process of submitting your financial information anyway. The PROFILE may ask both parties to contribute *more* than the FAFSA, but the difference should not be significant. FAFSA4caster is the quickest and easiest way to get an approximation of what the financial burden will be, regardless of where your child goes to college.

Filling out the FAFSA4caster takes about 30 minutes. You'll go online to fafsa.ed.gov, and you and your spouse, if you have one, will input your financial information. You'll also input your child's financial information, if he or she has any income or assets. The FAFSA4caster doesn't save your information or share it with anyone. You may create a profile with your email, but your actual names will not be on the form. As you fill it out, you may tell your children exactly what your financial situation is, or you may not. The beauty of FAFSA4caster is that you can fill it out with your child, and you don't have to share your income and assets if you don't want you to.

But you *will* learn what your expected family contribution, or EFC, is. It's important for your child to understand how much you and your spouse are expected to be able to pay for college, because you may have to make some changes as a family in order to afford it.

At the end of FAFSA4caster, you can choose to compare the average cost of a private education to the average cost of a public education, in or out of state. When you submit the FAFSA4caster, it'll give you a summary page. Your EFC will be at the middle of the page under "Difference" and you will have to pick a college, enter the total cost of attendance (use College Navigator), and it will automatically fill in a work-study income and $5,500 in Direct loans, which is the maximum freshmen can take. It'll be anywhere from 0 to 999,999; this is the dollar amount that you and your spouse should be able to pay out of pocket (from savings, income from assets, or discretionary income). Write this number down on a separate sheet of paper. This is the most useful part of the FAFSA and the most germane to this chapter.

Above the EFC is a chart that estimates the amount your child could theoretically get in federal aid. It includes loans, and Pell if you're eligible. We're not thrilled with this part of the FAFSA4caster; it tends to allow families to make an assumption, based on the FAFSA4caster estimate, of what the aid and loans will be—and it never looks like enough. Remember: The FAFSA4caster aid estimate is *only federal*—it does not estimate what your child might get in need- or merit-based aid from a specific college or university or grants from your home state.

As you can see from your summary, FAFSA will subtract the grants and loans that your child is likely eligible for from the average cost of tuition, and show you an estimated gap at the bottom of the page. Please bear in mind that the cost of tuition used by FAFSA is an average *sticker* price; it doesn't use data based on what families actually pay, just what colleges and universities report that they *charge*. For more information about sticker price and net price, see Chapter 7.

The FAFSA4caster may have awarded your child up to $9,000 or more in loans (two Direct loans and a Perkins, if you're eligible).

Your child *does not* have to take out these loans, and *you should not use them to meet your EFC*. The EFC is a family responsibility; student loans will be your child's (for federal loans, you will not sign on as a cosigner—the responsibility will be entirely your child's), and your child will use them to meet his or her need (direct costs – EFC = your child's need). We're not against loans; a reasonable amount of student loans can help build credit and responsible financial behaviors, and ultimately, your child, the person who is receiving the education, should be responsible for paying for as much of it as he or she can. But as we discussed in Chapter 3, student loans can easily become unreasonable—and unmanageable. Take out your sheet of paper, where you've already written down your EFC. Next to that, write down the amount in loans that FAFSA4caster predicts your child will be eligible for.

Step 2: Understanding student loan burdens

When we outlined this step for your child, we encouraged the child to go online to Finaid.org and use the Finaid student loan calculator to calculate what the monthly payments might be, and then discuss those with you. Although it may seem premature, the one drawback of FAFSA4caster is that it automatically calculates an estimate of your federal loan eligibility, and in that sense, it's front-loading the conversation with an assumption of student loan debt. So before you start making decisions about how much funding will come from loans, you should have a basic conversation about loans with your child and calculate the repayment. The college, and the federal government, will do this as well—but *after* your child has applied and been accepted. At that point, it's too late to change your mind. What is your child going to do? Withdraw the application 10 days before class starts and spend another year at home? Of course not. So it's good to have this conversation now, and it will allow you to understand the various aid awards you will receive from colleges much more efficiently. So ask yourself and your spouse the following question: How much do you think your child should take out in loans? Although tuition costs have risen enormously—faster than healthcare and any other section of the economy—that doesn't necessarily mean that the *value* of a degree has risen enormously. Before you commit to a final answer, if you're encouraging your child to take on more loans (we consider anything more than $32,000 in total debt for four years, or roughly $320 per month on a 10-year repayment plan, to be truly unreasonable for any college graduate) and perhaps to attend a college where he is *not* in the top 25 percent of applicants (a more competitive school where they may receive significantly less aid), please think about the following.

An undergraduate degree is not the same as medical school or law school; that is, there is no guarantee that upon graduation your child will have a high-paying job. To put it bluntly, undergraduate degrees are no longer a money-making enterprise; they have become as requisite as a high school diploma (and in some fields, about as valuable). And if your child is interested in a career in business, law, medicine, science, mathematics, or any other traditionally high-paying field, she will likely need to go to graduate school for an MBA, a JD, an MD, or a PhD. That means your child will need to have some borrowing capacity when she graduates from college; if she takes on too much in debt for undergrad, she won't be able to afford graduate school.

We've each been in the business of college admission and financial aid for more than 40 years. We've worked with nearly a hundred colleges and universities, and personally hired at least several hundred employees between us. The previous statement we made about the value of a college degree is our opinion, and we've formed it from our experiences in both the industry of higher education *and* as employers. It's certainly possible to find statistics on the web that claim college graduates make more than a million dollars in extra income throughout the course of their lifetimes. Here's what we have to say about those statistics: They're generally true—*for engineers*. Engineers of any stripe skew compensation data greatly. So if your child is incredible at math or science—and plans on attending an engineering school such as MIT, RPI, Harvey Mudd, or Union—he can usually count on making lots of money. But if your child is at all interested in the humanities, the nonprofit sector, teaching, development, politics, or essentially any other career that does not involve being a wizard with numbers—the smartest financial decision he can make is to keep his college debt as low as possible, so that he can take any kind of job he would like to, no matter how low-paying an entry-level position in his chosen field might be.

There's also the issue of where, and how, your child will live after college. We discuss this extensively in Chapter 3; if you haven't read it, we can sum it up quickly. From your perspective, it's fairly simple: Your child is about to move out of the house. You do not want her to move back home after she graduates. She will leave her stuff everywhere, drink all your wine, drive your cars, drain your wallets, and most importantly, she won't be leading her own life. We've both become empty-nesters and it is *wonderful*. Don't get us wrong; we love our children and we love having them around. We really love it when they visit. But as empty-nesters, we run around naked, we eat whatever we want, we don't watch our language, and we spend our money on ourselves. If we want to spend three days doing nothing but going to the gym, doing work, hanging out with our spouses, and eating takeout, we can. It's a return to the life we had before we had children, when we had zero responsibilities. Remember that time? Wasn't it amazing? You can be back there! Just don't let your children take on so much student loan debt that they have to move back home with you. As an added benefit, watching our children become smart, successful adults who we consider our friends and peers has been exceptional.

Step 3: Meeting the EFC

It's entirely possible that you looked at your EFC, as calculated by FAFSA4caster, and thought, "That's all?" If that happened to you, then multiply your EFC by 1.5; having that extra money budgeted may mean the difference between your child attending a school where she is funded (and she's in the top 25 percent of the academic class), and one that's more competitive, where she's *not* in the top 25 percent of the class. If she's not in the top quartile, you'll likely have to shell out more money in order to make up the difference. If your child is in the middle 50 percent of applicants at a more competitive college, she'll probably get *some* aid, but not a lot; and having that extra .5 of your EFC may be the key to sending her to that kind of school.

We're going to guess, however, that you did not look at the EFC and think, "No big deal!" It's much more likely that you looked at it and thought, "What on earth? Where am I supposed to find that kind of money?" As we said in Chapter 2, the EFC can look like an astronomical amount of money. There's one easy way to break it down, however; most colleges will allow you to pay your EFC in a 10-month payment plan. So start off by dividing the EFC by 10. You'll need to meet that monthly payment for 10 months out of the year, each year your child is in school.

If you've put aside any funds in a 529 savings plan, a Coverdell ESA (also known as an Educational IRA), mutual funds, or savings bonds, use those funds to meet your EFC. We recommend dividing the total by four, and using part of those savings each year, instead of spending it all on their first year or two.

If you've still got a few years before your child enrolls in college, and you haven't begun saving, you should *start saving tomorrow*. It's *always* cheaper to save than it is to borrow, and the sooner you become used to taking a cut from your paycheck before you calculate your discretionary income, the easier it will be to meet your EFC. *Here's a quick breakdown on the most common types of college savings plans* (they should be available through your bank or any financial services you use, like Charles Schwab or Ameriprise):

- **529 Savings Plans:** Also known as a "qualified tuition plan," 529s are a tax-advantaged plan designed expressly to save for college costs, and are authorized by Section 529 of the IRS tax code. If you know, without a doubt, where your child will be attending college, it's possible to use a 529 as a *prepaid tuition plan*; this will lock in tuition prices at eligible public and private universities. Credits purchased in a prepaid plan will always keep their value—for example, a half-year's tuition will *always* be a half-year's tuition, no matter how much the actual dollar cost increases. For public universities, every state, including Washington, D.C., has one; private colleges use the Private College 529 program, which currently has about 300 colleges (and you can use the credits at any of these schools). For participating schools and more information, go to privatecollege529.com. And because it's often difficult to predict where your child would like to go to school, another option is to open a 529 as a college savings plan, instead of a prepaid tuition plan. You can use a 529 savings plan at any college, for any education-related expense (including books, room and board, fees, and computers). Earnings in 529 savings plans are tax-exempt; total contributions in many states cannot exceed $300,000. For more information about your home state's 529 plans, please see our website at thefinancialaidhandbook.com.

- **Coverdell ESA:** A Coverdell ESA, also known as an Educational IRA, is like a small IRA (independent retirement account), without some of the tax benefits. Annual contributions cannot exceed $2,000, and are not tax-deductible, but earnings and distributions are tax-free.

- **Roth IRA:** A Roth IRA isn't the *best* way to save for college, but the laws allowing tax-free withdrawals of contributions can benefit you if an emergency arises and you need to put some of the funds toward something else. A Roth is commonly invested in mutual funds.

If you withdraw funds from a 529 or Coverdell account for any purpose other than education, you'll be subject to a 10 percent tax penalty.

The final word on saving for college

We recommend investing in a 60/20/20 mix of 529 savings/ Coverdell/Roth IRA. This allows you to retain a small portion of penalty-free assets in a Roth should an emergency arise, and to create, if the funds go unused, a starter retirement account for your child or even a penalty-free down payment contribution to a first home. Because of the recent economic trend in transitions from employer-paid and vested traditional benefit-defined retirement funds to 401ks and IRAs, and the emergence of a truly global-free market that relies heavily on freelancers and independent contractors, a small starter Roth can make an enormous difference in the long-term economic well-being of your child, and provide a small safety net of assets for you if your financial circumstances change.

If you haven't saved enough or at all

If you haven't set aside savings for your child's education, the easiest way to begin meeting your EFC is to adjust your spending. That may mean some serious shifts in the way you live, and we understand exactly how difficult that is. We recommend, however, that you adjust your spending first, and think about borrowing as a last resort.

Why you need to meet your EFC using current income

Your assets may not have any value

Let's start with home equity. It's likely that your adulthood has been a time of fluctuating credit during which you saw your investment in your home move from something you considered *a place to live* into an erstwhile ATM, whose equity loans allowed you to pull the credit lever at-will. You may have used home equity to upgrade your home, for travel, for the purchase of a second home, for a boat, new cars, or consumer goods. That vanished briefly in 2008, but it's also likely that you can do that again: Home equity has made a comeback. The lesson we all learned is to *cautiously* use that equity, and remember that what goes up will go down.

If they do have value, it has declined

Even outside the housing market, the pre-crash market contained other economic oddities that likely influenced your long-term spending habits. As we said earlier, retirement funds, which morphed from employer-paid and vested traditional benefit-defined pension funds, became 401ks and IRAs, which all boomed in value throughout the past 20 years—until, of course, they nose-dived. Too many of us (and yes, that includes us, although we may be 20 or 30 years your senior) became accustomed to looking at our quarterly 401k statements and assuming we *actually had that amount of money in hand.* And now, although many of us have enjoyed a full recovery, we definitely need to consider those assets as tools for the reason we participated in those programs to begin with: retirement.

You already make enough money—you're just spending it on garbage

We've come to the crux of most spending habits: the issue of *stuff*. Thanks to a globalized free market that brought both durable consumer goods and our endless appetite for acquisition to our doorsteps and laptop screens, we began purchasing things we didn't need by the bucket (or by the cardboard box from Amazon). Think about all the crap in your house. How many iPods do you have? Cell phones? Laptops? Clothing? Cable? Televisions? iPads? DVD and Blu-Ray players? It really is just *crap* that you don't need, but you're probably used to the drain on your bank account and can't imagine living without at least a little bit of retail therapy. And it used to be easy; getting credit was a piece of cake, and your investments looked sound. That's probably not true for you anymore. So you know what? Get rid of all your crap! Sell it on eBay. Use that digital camera you bought and only take out once a year, put your crap against a white background, and get rid of as much of it as you can handle. It might not bring you a huge windfall, but it *will* get it out of your house. Getting it out of the house is important; crap is kind of like animals. You have to keep feeding them. New expensive parts for the expensive car; new everything for the boat; new hair cream to offset the damage you did with a new hair dryer, and so on. Buying and maintaining your stuff is an enormous waste of time and money.

You, at this point, are either thinking "Yes! I am ready for a moratorium on stuff and spending! Let's clean house! I've been waiting for an excuse to free myself of my earthly possessions!" or "Why should I get rid of the things I work so hard for so that my entitled teenager can go learn about Marx, edibles, vape culture, partially shaved haircuts, hand tattoos, Judith Butler, volunteer organic farming, and DIY music festivals for four years? If she wants to do that, she can pay for it herself."

We're guessing that it's the latter. We have one answer for you: *It's the economy.*

The difference in the economy from the time that you entered the workforce and when your child will be graduating from college could be measured in light years. *This is not just about the recent recession. The last 10 to 20 years have altered the way we do business in America and in the world. Forever.* Advances in technology meant the development of a truly global business environment. In simple English, that means the internet. The internet is not just a revolution for consumers and communicators; it has absolutely revolutionized *business*. Every single kind of business. The dot-com bubble in the early 2000s was almost a joke compared to the amount of money that the internet has enabled the *entire* economy to make. Since the commercialization of the internet in the mid-1990s, our GDP, or gross domestic product, has increased by nearly 9 trillion dollars—more than *doubling* in size. That means that in the last 20 years, we've more than doubled the wealth in the United States—and it could not, would not, have happened without the internet. When it comes to understanding the importance of the internet's impact on every part of the workforce, we're not talking about Twitter or Facebook. We're talking about real tools, everything from Skype to GoogleDocs, which allow people to do business efficiently and meaningfully, from anywhere. Those tools simply did not exist when you graduated from high school; today's economy is completely different. It's one where the best, the brightest, and—most importantly—the *most agile* will be the ones to succeed.

The hemorrhage of jobs we experienced in the beginning of this decade also pushed millions of people into an economy where they would take whatever work they could get, further cementing a pattern of globalized freelancers. Businesses that survived our last recession have come to rely on, and profit from, a contractor-based business model that simply would not have been possible 15 years ago. What does that mean? It means, quite simply, that job security as we knew it is no longer a safe bet. The new economy means that many of the assumptions we've had as adults about the workplace flew out the window. High-paying jobs with benefits, pensions, and job security for decades are becoming extinct.

Your children will be graduating from college into a world without defined benefit pension funds or high-paying starting salaries. The declining size of their generation against a peak growth period of 15 years means that the competition will ease a bit over recent times; there will be roughly 2 percent fewer graduates of the high school class of 2023 than there were in 2010. They won't struggle as dramatically as their older siblings and friends to find internships and likely won't have to take as many low-paying jobs to get their feet in the door, but it will still be challenging to gain a sure-footed hold on their careers after graduation. Asking your children to take on an unreasonable amount of debt will only handicap them. An excess of debt for an education they cannot afford, in an economy that is still uncertain, could make your child's education a moot point—or even a negative-sum game.

Whether your own experiences have you nodding your head in agreement, or shaking it in disbelief, we want you to take away one thing that we think everyone can agree on: *It's always important to be conservative about borrowing.* Asking your children to take on too much student debt, either because you don't want to pay your EFC, or because you think they should go to a "better" school, where they receive no funding, is a bad idea. The most important skills your children can have in this economy—one where big companies and big names are often the *least* effective—are not about the brand name of their college or university. Brand is not a skill; it might be an asset, but it won't outweigh the burden of too many student loans. What your child will need is the ability to learn quickly, communicate beautifully, collaborate with ease, and understand and master changes in technology, no matter what the field. It's that simple. Although we've said it before, we'll say it again. *No one really cares about undergraduate*; it is not law school or medical school. It does not necessarily "pay you back," but it *is* something that your children absolutely have to do, just like high school was for you.

In 2023, when your child will enter the workforce, there will be more jobs for college-educated workers than for those without a college degree—even with, or perhaps especially because of, the 2008 crash. According to a 2016 study from the Georgetown University Center on Education and the Workforce, 95 percent of the 11.6 million new jobs created in the economic recovery went to people with some college education. Your children *must* go to college. They should go to a school that's a great fit for them; one that challenges them intellectually and offers them a scholarship. It's that simple. But even if your child gets the best scholarship their dream school has to offer, the college may still expect you to meet your EFC. If you pass the burden of the EFC down to your child, you will absolutely be disadvantaging them in the job market after they graduate. You will be *paralyzing* your child. Don't do it. *Find a way to meet the EFC.*

We genuinely believe that investing in your child's education is a worthy endeavor; it's far more valuable to you, as a parent, than dinners out, club memberships, or the latest model automobile. And we personally believe that there is, other than our own retirement funds, no better place we can spend our money than on our children's education. This doesn't mean that you should mortgage your house and your future to send Susie to her dream school, nor does it mean that you should borrow or sacrifice in order to maintain a certain lifestyle for your child. Susie doesn't need a daily on-campus latte, a shopping trip, or spring break in Cancun, no matter how much she might want those things, and if she can't get a scholarship, she doesn't need a big-brand school. But she will need you to meet your EFC.

Where do I start?

You and your spouse should go through the following itemizations of how you spend your combined after-tax income:

- Monthly mortgage payments or rent.
- Utilities.
- Food.
- Household insurance.
- Property or school tax.
- Health insurance.
- Retirement contributions and savings.
- Consumer debt.
- Transportation (including car payments, insurance, and gas).
- Care for your other children, if you have them.
- Any other necessary costs, like caring for an aging parent or disabled child.

Those are your financial priorities; anything else, such as vacations or large consumer purchases, are unnecessary. Although you've probably talked about it in the past, you and your spouse will want to discuss any assumptions you might be making about your own jobs or incomes, and any concerns you might have about your individual situations. That means potential layoffs at your place of work, mandatory furloughs, financial support for either of your own parents, commitments either one of you may have made to members of your blended family (including alimony and child support), and how long you have until your next child (if you have one) enters college.

If you're planning for multiple college tuitions, don't forget to tell FAFSA4caster (and re-calculate your EFC, if needed). Your portion of the EFC will change when you have two kids in college simultaneously—it gets divided in half, then for three children in thirds, and so on. Your children's assets and income will count only toward their own EFC. To plan, try using a laddergram like the one shown here:

EFC with one child in college: $10,000

EFC with two children in college: $5,000

EFC with three children in college: $3,333

	2017	2018	2019	2020	2021	2022	2023	2024
William	$10,000	$10,000	$5,000	$5,000				
Barbara			$5,000	$5,000	$3,333	$3,333		
Susie					$3,333	$3,333	$5,000	$5,000
Krista					$3,333	$3,333	$5,000	$5,000

After subtracting your financial priorities from your monthly take-home incomes, you might discover that you have a few hundred, or even thousand, extra dollars. Where does it all go? We're willing to bet it goes to small things, such as $5 lattes, $6 half-gallons of fresh-squeezed juice, new clothes, movie tickets, vacations, and so on. If your bank allows online banking—and most of us use it—log online *right now* and set up an automatic transfer for payday, and put at least half of the extra in a savings or money market account. If you can put aside $500 with each biweekly paycheck, that's $12,500 per year (or $13,500 per year if you work all 52 weeks), and $1,000 per biweekly paycheck is a cool $25,000.

Another way to calculate is to take your EFC and divide it by 25 (half the working weeks in the year, and the number of paychecks you'll receive). That will give you exactly the number you need to auto-save from each paycheck.

But it's more likely that you've subtracted your financial priorities from your take-home pay, and come up with bupkis—or worse, a negative number. If you've got assets or savings that you've ear-marked for your retirement, don't even consider touching them. We do not recommend that you cash in on, or borrow against, your own future. If you can't support yourself in retirement, the burden will fall on your child. What you'll need to do now is look at your list of financial priorities, and see where you can make changes. Go down the list, item by item, and discuss ways to cut back. We've got two important bills that we'd like you to consider first.

The #1 drain on family finances: cars!

How many cars do you have? How much do they cost you?

Oh, we could rail against cars all day. It has nothing to do with their environmental impact, either. It's simple: Cars only depreci-ate in value. From the perspective of any financial planner, cars are infuriating. They are worth significantly less from the moment you drive them off the lot.

Think about it this way: If you were dealing with the stock mar-ket, you would never, ever want to invest in something that only loses value. It's not like you think that someday, your brand-new Suburban is going to skyrocket in value. You KNOW it will decline in value, and yet, people continue to buy new cars. Why? It's such a waste of money! When you buy a brand-new car, you're a sucker. You've been tricked. Your car is a living, breathing, four-wheeled money pit. Gas, insurance, and monthly car payments can run you several thousand dollars a month . . . or they can run you a couple of hundred dollars a month. It's up to you.

So what can you do? Honestly, sell your cars to pay off your auto loans, and buy a used car that has lots of airbags. Or get a bicycle and use public transit (we know this isn't an option for most people, but hey, think about it anyway). Don't spend more than $15,000 on your "new" used car, and try to get a certified one—most car manufacturers will inspect their used cars so that you know they're not lemons.

You might be reluctant to do this. Don't be! Your car is an expensive ball and chain! Free yourself of it today.

If you're still unwilling to get rid of your car, try this: Take the amount of discretionary income you calculated earlier, and add the dollar cost of your car(s) to it. Look! You could have so much more money each month! It's possible that you wouldn't need to change a single thing about your finances, if you just could *keep* the money you normally spend on cars.

Your home expenses

Other than your basic utilities—heating, cooling, gas, water, electric, and maintenance costs—how much do you spend on cable television and phone bills? Add up the total costs, and then get ready to start subtracting. Begin by getting rid of your cable TV; you can watch everything you need to on Hulu or Netflix for $10 per month. Does everyone need a smartphone with unlimited data? Or even at all? Can you charge any of the bills to your employer? If you're willing to get rid of or greatly reduce these costs, you could have an extra $250 (or more) per month.

For more detailed and creative ways to reduce your spending, check out one or more of the following:

- Suze Orman's *Action Plan: New Rules for New Times*, or suzeorman.com.
- Chris Farrell's *The New Frugality.*
- Mary Hunt's "The Everyday Cheapskate" newsletter; sign up at debtproofliving.com.
- Dave Ramsey's *The Total Money Makeover.*

Borrowing to meet your EFC

Although we strongly recommend that you significantly reduce your spending in order to meet your EFC, sometimes it's not possible. You may also need some additional funds to help your child if he or she doesn't get the highest possible aid award. *You can take out a federally-backed student loan for yourself.* Parent PLUS loans are like Direct loans for adults; they're federally guaranteed loans with a fixed interest rate of 6.31 percent. They can only be used for educational expenses, and interest is charged from the day you take out the loan. The actual dollars will be given directly to the college, which will then disburse the funds, typically twice a year. They'll use the funds for tuition, room and board, and any other direct fees, then give the remainder to you in a check. You can authorize any part or all of the remainder into your child's account at the school, if you so desire and expressly authorize it. The amount you can take out is directly tied to your student's aid award and the college's cost of attendance:

College's cost of attendance – Your child's financial aid award = The amount you're eligible to take out in PLUS Loans each year

If you're not eligible for PLUS loans, your child may take out more than the standard limits for a Direct Stafford—up to $12,500 per year. We do not recommend exceeding the standard Direct Stafford loan limit of $7,500 per year under any circumstance.

How much should you take out in PLUS loans?

Log on to Finaid.org and use the student loan calculator (you'll enter the interest at 6.31 percent) to calculate what your payments will be. Do the math; how much can you afford? When can you start paying it down? Will it interfere with any other debt you currently have? Don't take on a PLUS loan until you've done the math.

What if my child has their heart set on a particular school?

We do understand the impulse to give your child anything that he or she wants. But it's probably not possible for you to do it, no matter how much you might want to. The old adage that would have your child going to "the best college they can get into" doesn't apply anymore. Unless your child has a very, very good chance of getting accepted to an elite college that is need-blind, you're probably going to need a scholarship.

Several years ago, we heard a father in a focus group describe his willingness to do whatever he had to in order to pay for his daughter's "dream college." He said, "If she wants the moon, I'll find a way." That was before the economy changed—and we're not even sure it made sense then. As lovely as it was to hear someone who was so devoted to his child, we wanted to shake that father and shout, "Be sensible! Don't mortgage your own future!"

You'll have to talk to your child about the school in question and determine what his chances of getting aid are. If he's in the middle 50 percent of applicants, he will probably get *some* aid (we cover this more in-depth in Chapter 6). Would you be able to afford the gap without taking on unreasonable debt for yourself? If not, you'll need to tell your child not to apply. If he applies, he'll fall in love (and you might too!). It's like taking your child to a dog breeder, letting them play with month-old puppies, and then leaving—*sans* puppy. It's a bad idea that will only end in heartbreak.

Should I cosign for my child's loan? Do I have to?

You do not need to cosign on a federal loan (Direct loan or Perkins). You can take out a private loan from a bank; there are a multitude of solutions from various lending companies. These loans can look fairly cheap, and they're easy enough to get if you've got a good credit rating. Go to studentlendinganalytics.com for completely independent and timely information about comparative rates. But beware of two things:

1. The minute you put your signature down as a cosigner, you're agreeing to repay the loan in full. If your child can't make the payments at any point, it will be your responsibility.
2. Unlike mortgages or car payments, many private student loans can't even be discharged through illness or death. If you cosign and your child becomes disabled or dies, you'll still be fully responsible for the loan.

Consider purchasing a form of credit insurance to protect you, should the worst happen.

Can anyone else cosign my child's loan?

Is there someone else in your family who would want to function as
the cosigner? We advocate this only if cosigning, and perhaps having to repay the loan, wouldn't jeopardize that person's financial
security. If your parents are on a fixed income, for example, they're
probably not the right people to ask. But your millionaire playboy
brother who doesn't have any children of his own? Ask him!

Talking to your child about your actual EFC

After you've gone through your finances, it's possible that you
won't be able to meet your full EFC, either each year, or for all four
years. Throughout the rest of the book, we'll refer to the amount
of the EFC that you can actually afford to pay as your *Actual EFC*.
You'll need to take note of the difference between your EFC and
your Actual EFC. Ultimately, it's your responsibility to make up the
difference, but if you can't you'll need to talk to your child about
what you can afford. We understand that it's difficult to say to your
children that you can't afford something. It's impossible for all of
us not to have some sense of self-worth tied into our annual earnings; whether we work in the profit or non-profit sector, income is
seen as a proxy for personal value. So try to think of this conversation as a variation on the traditional college talk: Instead of having
a "reach" and a "safety" school, you're going to ask your child to
apply only to schools where he or she will be *funded*.

Scripted Conversation Starters

If you need some help getting started, we've got a few ideas:

Thanks for making the time to sit down and talk with us.
We know this isn't on your top 10 list of things to do, but

we want to let you know how proud we are of what you've accomplished in school. We want to support you in college, but there are some limits to that. We've done a thorough review of our finances, and we know that we can provide [your Actual EFC] amount for you each year, so you'll need to go to a college where you can get enough in aid to make up the difference.

———

Here's how much we can spend. Here are our reasons; we have to pay for [these other things], and while your education is important to us, those other expenditures are non-negotiable. We'd like you to keep that in mind as you look at colleges, and only apply to schools where you'll be in the top 25 percent of applicants. Although we can't give you more money, we'd love to give you our time, and help you look for schools and work on your applications.

———

We don't want you to graduate from college with a crippling loan burden. Although we can give you [your Actual EFC, if it's larger than the EFC] per year, a portion of that will need to replace some of the loans you would be eligible for with a financial aid package. That means you'll need to get merit aid; it's important to us that you'll be able to afford to live on your own after you graduate.

———

We love you and we're so excited that you're ready for college, but your siblings also need to go through school. We've gone through our finances, and we can give you each [your Actual EFC]. We'll need you to give your car to your sister, and get a summer job to help cover costs. If you'd like to go anywhere besides [a local public or community college that you could pay for out of pocket], you will need a scholarship.

For divorced and/or blended families

If you're planning on getting remarried, we recommend that you have a discussion about the financial implications of remarriage and college cost with your fiancé(e). If you remarry, your new spouse's assets and income will also be considered in the FAFSA. That means your spouse will be equally responsible for your child's college education, and his or her income will raise your EFC. Is your soon-to-be-spouse willing to take on this responsibility? If not, you need to have a serious discussion about this, and consider putting off your wedding until your children have graduated from college. These are modern times!

If you've already remarried, bear in mind that your spouse's finances will be calculated in the FAFSA and PROFILE. If, when you remarry, you signed a pre-nuptial agreement that precludes the stepparent from paying for any of your child's college education, that agreement is void; the reason is that two parties cannot make an agreement that binds a third party (in this case, the third party is the federal government). If you're the custodial parent, your spouse is required by law to include his or her assets in the FAFSA. If, however, the financial obligations of that stepparent include other college tuitions, that obligation will be included in the FAFSA the same way that any legal siblings (blood relatives or adopted siblings) would be. If those step-siblings consider the custodial stepparent to be *their* non-custodial parent, their information won't be included (but all alimony and paid child support will be).

If you need to discuss this with an estranged spouse, we recommend that you move beyond any petty grievances you might have, and arrange a time to talk. Ask him or her to split the EFC with you.

Be prepared for this discussion; get ready to talk about the FAFSA, what you can contribute, and what your child might otherwise need from the other parent. Be willing to create a deal sheet that lists commitments for both parties, and sign off on it at the end of the conversation (full names and a date).

If prior experience with your ex leads you to believe that there's no chance for a positive or productive discussion between the two of you, consider the following alternatives:

- Has there been a neutral party (pastor, social worker, accountant) who has helped you in discussions of your child on previous occasions?
- Can you hire a mediator? We recommend this if you know that your ex has the financial ability to help your child with college.
- If all else fails, would you be willing to consult the attorney that represented you in your divorce? Remember: Your attorney is paid to be your advocate, and your child's education is a priority. If you can spend enough on an attorney to come to an agreement about the next four years, it might be worth the headache.

What if my former spouse is a deadbeat or otherwise absent?

You'll have to talk with each college about this individually, but don't worry: All colleges and universities have a protocol for this. Your ex is not the first—nor will he or she be the last—to "decline to participate." You'll have to get a waiver of non-custodial information; be prepared to document all conversations and other evidence of refusal, such as missed child support payments or alimony, for the college itself.

What else can I do?

Read through our next chapter and learn how you can help your child look for colleges at which he or she has a high chance of getting aid. Help your child with their applications, and visit two or three of the top contenders. After applications are submitted, you'll file your taxes as soon as you can, then file the FAFSA, which you can do as early as January 1 of the year of enrollment.

6

Merit Aid and
The MAP

MERIT AID IS part of your financial aid award; it will be awarded
to you after you've already applied to colleges. If you apply to the
right schools, you'll likely get enough merit and need-based aid to
make your education affordable. In this chapter, we explain how
merit aid is awarded, and how you can determine whether or not
you're a good candidate for it, and at what colleges, using our MAP,
or Merit Aid Profile. You're going to define yourself in this chapter;
not just through your grades, but through your extracurriculars
and interests.

What, exactly, is merit aid?

Merit aid, also known as gift aid, a tuition discount, a college scholarship, or an institutional grant, is what you will receive if you're
in the top 25 percent (or even 50 percent) of the incoming class at
most colleges. Merit aid, put simply, is free money. You don't have
to repay it. It can take the form of actual cash that the college will
disburse to you, or simply be reflected in a discounted tuition rate.

Merit aid is a *real* college scholarship; it comes from the college itself, and is usually significantly larger than any outside, or private, scholarship you could receive.

Colleges and universities give out merit aid for one simple reason: to get the students they want the most. Only about 30 percent of all full-time students pay the full sticker price of tuition, room and board, and fees; the remaining 70 percent receive some kind of discount right off the top, whether it's through federal loans, grants, work-study, or merit aid.[1] As we mentioned in Chapter 1, tuition is a mutable, changeable thing, which changes based entirely on how much the college wants the student to enroll. Many colleges use the bottom 50 percent of the incoming class to pay for the top 50 percent of the incoming class.

Why do colleges discount their tuition? What's the point?

You might wonder: If colleges are discounting their tuition for 70 percent of students on average, why not just *lower the price of tuition*? Well, that's because from the remaining 30 percent, they're getting the highest possible price. It's in the college's best interest, however odd it may seem, to use a high sticker price overall. Colleges use a process known as "leveraging," a form of economic and statistical modeling, to determine *exactly* how much money they have to give you in order to get you to enroll—no more, no less. Sticker price also positions the college in the market, and can make them appear to be a "better," or more selective, school. It's like a department store; the retail price determines what section your product will be in. An $8,000 dress won't be placed in the "juniors" section at Bloomingdale's along with prom dresses—it will be on the top floor, with high-end designers (whether or not it *comes* from a high-end designer).

A great example of sticker-price placement is Boston University. BU is a large private university located in central Boston with an enrollment of more than 17,000 undergraduates, according to the College Board, and it accepts 33 percent of applicants. BU's self-reported cost of attendance for 2016–17 is $68,060. It has a sophisticated website whose colors—maroon and white—are rather reminiscent of another local college: Harvard University.

If you had to ask a group of your friends, "Which school is better—Harvard or BU?" they would likely answer "Harvard" without a second thought. That's the *perceived value* of a Harvard degree; their brand presence is exceptional. If you calculate the lifetime return on investment (ROI), or the actual possible dollar value of the degree, as PayScale.com did in 2016, you'd discover that Harvard *is* a great school, coming in at #22 on the list. The Harvard graduate averages $739,000 at that position. (Caltech and MIT are in positions 1 and 2, respectively, for the highest lifetime dollar return on investment.)

On that same list, Boston University clocked in at #298 with a lifetime ROI of $383,000 dollars. So when we think about those two indexes of value—perception and documented financial value—Harvard is, by far, the better school. That's not a surprise. But what *is* a surprise is Harvard's cost of attendance for 2015–16: $64,400. Harvard is *less expensive* than BU at $65,900 for 2015–16. Why is BU *more* expensive? Because it wants to be perceived as being *as good as Harvard*; it wants to be perceived as a highly selective elite college, even though its acceptance rates (33 percent of all applicants) are nowhere near as selective as Harvard's (only 6 percent).[2] No matter how you cut it, BU is not Harvard—but it would like to *appear* to be, by charging the same amount or more.

Expensive, but less selective, large private schools like BU and NYU, which we discussed in the first chapter, are great places to get a good education. They have wonderful faculty, great course offerings, and engaged student life. But if you can't pay outright for them, or be in the top 25 percent of applicants and receive enough in aid, they are not worth borrowing to attend. It's not a logical financial risk; no matter how much they might emulate top-tier elite colleges, they just aren't. You will not see the same financial reward—but their sticker price, higher than Harvard or even Yale, implies that you *could*. It's a pricing trick. Don't fall for it.

This isn't necessarily a bad thing. It's just the way the market works. Universities are, at the end of the day, businesses. So while it doesn't do any good to complain about unfair pricing policies, it does help you to understand that at any given college, if you're not in at least the top 50 percent of the incoming class, and you're not poor enough to have an EFC that's low enough for Pell, the university in question may have absolutely no interest in funding you.

So where can I get merit aid?

After you apply, each college that gives you an offer of admission will also, hopefully, give you a financial aid offer. That financial aid award will be made up of both need-based (what gets calculated by the FAFSA and PROFILE) and merit-based aid. Most colleges and universities hand out their aid dollars sequentially; they start with the top 5 percent of applicants, then move onto the top 10 percent, then 15 percent, and so on. The top 5 percent is often the top-fifth *academic* percentile, but not always. Different colleges have different priorities; that's where your extracurriculars and interests come in to play. They might award their need and merit dollars to students who are affiliated with the same religious organization as the college, students who have exceptional volunteer résumés, or students who are interested in digital media. It just depends on the college. Most colleges and universities cannot afford to give need-based aid to all of their students. For more information about need, the EFC, and the COA, turn to Chapter 2.

Colleges that *don't* give merit aid are usually need-blind and meet full need, and they don't give merit aid because they don't have to. Those colleges are generally incredibly selective, and although many of them do meet full need if they accept you, your family may still not be able to afford it. For many middle-class families, the EFC (what the family is required to pay) is still high enough that paying it outright represents a real financial sacrifice. Although it may look to the government as though your family has the assets on hand, many families do not. There's a multitude of reasons for this. Job loss, asset loss (from the devaluation of investments), home foreclosure, and other expenses, such as caring for a disabled child or elderly parent, are just a few. So if you're accepted to an incredibly selective college that will meet your full need (COA-EFC), but you still can't pay a large part of your EFC, we recommend that you also apply to other schools that disburse merit aid in addition to need-based aid.

Finding merit aid is tricky. It's not recorded on any single website or in any single book. The reasons for this have to do with data reporting. Although colleges and universities report their data to various agencies, including the federal government, *U.S. News & World Report,* The College Board, Petersen's, NACUBO, and so on, much of this reporting isn't useful to anyone other than the requestor, and no single source gathers detailed enough information on aid policies. The next time we have a million dollars and a team of statisticians, we'd love to give it a shot—but for now, and likely the next decade, that data won't be available. Admission data and freshman class profiles, however, are *always* reported, and they're widely available for free and online, from the College Board (bigfuture.collegeboard.org) and IPEDS (nces.ed.gov/ipeds). We can also find out from those same sources how much a single college gives away in aid, and how much on average; when we compare this to their freshman class profile, you can make an educated guess about how much any given student might receive in aid.

Because most colleges award their aid dollars by funding the best and brightest of their applicants *first* (however they define that—it may be through grades, extracurriculars, talent, or organizational affiliation), you have the highest possible chance of receiving a scholarship if you're in the top 25 percent of the incoming freshman class. If you're in the middle 50 percent of applicants, you will likely get *some* aid, but possibly not enough, unless your financial need is significant.

We've made some assumptions about you, audience. We're willing to bet that most of you are middle-class kids with great, but not spectacular, grades; you'll qualify for financial aid, but not Pell. That means you're the average applicant. If your grades and test scores put you above and beyond the average applicant, and your EFC is incredibly low (Pell or lower; go to studentaid .ed.gov to find out more), it's not unreasonable for you to apply to a need-blind college that meets full need, such as an Ivy or Little Ivy, where you will likely get enough in need-based aid to make college affordable for you. But for everyone else—whose family might be able to just barely meet their EFC or not at all—we recommend that you apply to less-selective (read: less selective than an Ivy, not a place with open admission) private colleges and universities, or to a local public (not out-of-state; the costs of out-of-state publics are comparably high to privates, and they give less aid).

Based on our own experience those colleges might be schools you've never heard of. And that's *a lot* of colleges; out of the more than 4,400 colleges and universities in the United States, how many have you heard of? Probably a handful of schools that are local to your home state, and 20 to 50 highly competitive schools. But there are so many more wonderful places out there—you just have to start looking.

And that's not to say that more selective colleges don't offer merit aid; the medium and smaller-sized ones often do. Gonzaga University, for example, is a medium-size, private, Jesuit-affiliated liberal arts college in Spokane, Washington. It has a DI men's basketball team, and its name is quite well-known. In 2016–17, the cost of attendance was $53,310; the *average* institutional grant (their own money) was about $20,411; and the average merit-based grant was $12,659. The middle 50 percent of that freshman class (the 25th to the 75th percentile) scored between 1090 and 1290 on the combined SAT, and 50 percent of their students have a 3.75 GPA or higher. So how do you find out where you need to fall in order to get merit aid? It's simple; you need to be in the top 25 percent. Your individual SAT or ACT score should be higher than the top score of the middle 50 percent, putting you above the 75th percentile. For Gonzaga, that would be an SAT above 1280, and a GPA of at least 3.75; you should then qualify for, at the bare minimum, $12,000 in aid (the average), if not significantly more. If your scores are demonstrably higher than that—say, a 1450 SAT with a

3.95—it's likely that you'd get at least $20,000 from Gonzaga (half-tuition). At a less selective school, that last set of credentials could get you full tuition, and a discounted room and board, if not a full ride.

How will you know what the top 25 percent of the class is?

To find information about the top 25 percent of the class, you have a few options. Most colleges report their information to the College Board. Go to bigfuture.collegeboard.org, type in the college's name, and on its profile, click "Applying." You can then select the tab labeled "Academics and GPA," which will allow you to put in your information to see how you stack up. You'll see a cool set of charts; as you put in your information, green check marks or blocks will show you how your "numbers" compare. For example, if you type in "Whittier College" and then click on the "SAT and ACT" tab, a green bar will show you where your scores place you among Whittier's first-year class. It's visual, it's fast, and it gives you a quick and accurate sense of whether or not you are in the top 25 percent.

GPA is a little trickier on the bigfuture.collegeboard.org site. GPA is reported in "slices": 3.75 and above; 3.5–3.74; 3.25–3.49; 3.00–3.24; you get the idea. For Gonzaga, which we mentioned earlier, 50 percent of the class had a 3.75 GPA or above. Although it doesn't *always* align exactly, we can guesstimate by subtracting 3.75 from 4, and dividing the remainder of .25 in half, then adding it to the reported GPA—determining that the top 25 percent had a GPA of around 3.875 (3.75 plus .125, or half of .25) or above.

Here are a few other examples of GPA guesstimates, using the College Board's data:

- At Drew University in New Jersey, 43 percent had a 3.75 GPA or above, and overall, 76 percent had a GPA of 3.25 or above. We'd guesstimate that the top 25 percent had a GPA of 3.625 or above (3.25 plus .375, or half of .75).

- At Agnes Scott College in Georgia, 50 percent had a GPA of 3.75 or above. We'd wager that the top 25 percent had a GPA of 3.82 or above; we found that by dividing .25 by 34 (to discover the remaining percentage points), then multiplying the answer—roughly .007—by 10, to get .07. We added that .07 to 3.75, and got 3.82.
- At Pepperdine University in California, 39 percent had a GPA of 3.75 or higher. That's a pretty high number; Pepperdine is a fairly competitive school. We guesstimate that the top 25 percent of the class has at least a GPA of 3.9 or higher. That's easy math; divide .25 in half to get .125, and add it to 3.75. You'll get 3.875; we rounded up to 3.9, for a conservative estimate, because there are so many students in the top percentile.

Get to the point! What colleges are going to give you merit aid?

In the next chapter, we cover how to look for colleges that will fund you. But before you can start searching, you need to know who you are and what your strengths are. Stop by your school's guidance counselor and get a copy of your transcript, just for your own reference (it doesn't need to be sealed), then start filling out our MAP on the following pages. You can also print out a copy from our website, or make your own.

The MAP (Merit Aid Profile)

Your Stats

You'll need to start by defining your own stats, which consist of three things: your SAT, ACT (or both), and your cumulative GPA, on a 4.0 scale.

SAT:

ACT:

GPA:

If you only have the SAT and not the ACT, or vice versa, ask your high school guidance counselor about a concordance table. You can find a converter tool for "old" and "new" SAT and ACT on the College Board website.

Is there room for improvement? An SAT or ACT prep class costs about $200 to $500 up front, but they're well worth the investment. Do you have another year (or two) to bring up your GPA? Although you might be encouraged to take as many weighted (honors or AP courses) as possible, we recommend that you only do so if you're certain that you'll excel. If you're terrible at math, don't take AP calculus just to prove you can pass; take whatever regular senior math class is available, and try your best to get an A. Your high school guidance counselor is the best person you can ask to help you figure out how to improve your grades and test scores.

How much you can afford to pay

If you haven't already, you'll need to calculate your EFC—what it is, and how much of it your family can actually afford. For more information on this, turn to Chapter 4. Here, you'll put in your calculated EFC, and the Actual EFC, or how much you can afford to pay (if it's not the full amount).

EFC:

Actual EFC:

Your local public

Before you start looking at any other colleges, you should find out what the tuition costs at your local public are; they're often significantly less expensive than private colleges, and you may be able to live at home (which will subtract room and board, but add commuting costs). We're big champions of public education, but it isn't always great for students who aren't joiners. If you're going to go to your local public and live at home, you'll have to work twice as hard to participate in the college community; living off-campus can be difficult. So if you're a real joiner—you love clubs and organizations—a public college could be a place where you'll really excel. Community colleges are also an *amazing* way to pay very little out of pocket; if you can do two years at a local community college, get extraordinary grades, and then transfer, you might be able to afford a wider selection of schools.

My local U: $ per year

My local community college: $ per year

Local costs

Actual EFC × 4 = $

Local U × 4 = $

Local Community College × 2 = $

Subtract your Local U × 4 from your Actual EFC × 4, or your Local CC × 2 from your Actual EFC × 4. You might be pleasantly surprised at how much funding you have left over!

You don't have to stay near home, but it's always worth considering. We don't necessarily recommend applying to out-of-state public colleges; they statistically give out less aid, and you'll have to pay for room and board. Many states, however, have reciprocity with neighboring states, and qualifying residents of Washington, D.C., may receive in-state tuition at any public college in the country through the DCTAG initiative. If you live in the west, look at the Western Undergraduate Exchange program (WUE); for the Midwest, look at the Midwest Student Exchange Program. Students living in the southern states will want to check out the Academic Common Market Regional Contract Program for professional health care degrees, and finally, in the northeast, the New England Regional Student Program provides options for specific majors. Do an online search using any of the previously mentioned program names, or go to our website at thefinancial aidhandbook.com.

Your interests and extracurriculars

After you've defined your stats, you'll need to go over your interests and extracurriculars. This can mean a lot of things—anything from volunteer work to videos that you've posted on YouTube for a class project. It can include community activities through your church, temple, or even atheist's organization; involvement in school plays or sports; and after-school jobs or internships.

Fill out the following chart; rate yourself on a **1** to **5** scale, **1** being the least involved person that you know, and **5** being the most, for each activity. Don't worry if you can't fill every category—few students can! We just like to leave a little extra room. Ignore the "Buzzwords" column for now; you'll fill that in later.

Category	Description	Buzzwords	Points
Leadership Experiences			
Activities: Sports, Clubs, Performing Arts			
Honors and Awards, Recognitions			

Community Involvement, Service, Volunteer Work			
All Others, including Paid Work			

Every activity for which you've given yourself a **3** or higher is one that you'll want to use in your application, and you might want to seek out the faculty or adult advisors who oversaw those projects. Can they help you with a recommendation? How do they feel about their *own* alma mater? Would you consider going to that school? If you're interested in applying to a college that an adult in your life is an alumna of, it would be fantastic to have a recommendation from that person.

If you've rated yourself a **1** or **2** for any activity, is there a way to become more involved before you send off your applications? Think about it, and try to become more involved. Whether that means spearheading a new initiative (adding vegan baked goods to bake sales) or taking a leadership role, you should try to bring those **1**s and **2**s up to **3**s, **4**s, and **5**s. If you're not interested, then forget about them—and devote yourself fully to your other activities.

Colleges prioritize extracurriculars in the same way that they prioritize anything else. The ideal merit aid candidate has extracurriculars that align with the college's values. If you've got strong leadership experiences, for example, you'll want to apply to the kind of college that values strong leadership experiences. When your academic credentials are tied to other things that the college values—whether that be diversity, community service, or the arts—you have a profile that hits on all possible cylinders. It's not a guarantee at every single school, but more often than not, matching yourself to a college's values gives you, as a prospective student, a much better chance of having your application placed in the right stack. But how can you figure that out? You'll need to talk the talk—and learn how to discuss your experiences on an application within a specific context. Get a colored pen, and circle the experiences you rated yourself the highest on.

Defining your buzzwords

Again, when colleges determine what they value in a student, it's not just about test scores—it's also about "strategic priorities," or buzzwords. After you've evaluated your extracurriculars and interests, you'll need to learn how to define them through the eyes of colleges and universities.

In our consulting business, we've been responsible for helping to build the strategic profile and priorities for numerous colleges and universities. Like anything, it's not a perfect process, but we try to define the kinds of students that the colleges want—and to define the colleges themselves—using a list of buzzwords.

How do you find buzzwords?

Buzzwords will be on the college's website. Different colleges put them in different places on their sites. The most common places are:

- **Mission Statement:** Targeted at potential faculty, alumni, and other professional parties, this is typically *not* written for students. This is usually kind of pedantic and dull, but it's not without value.

- **About Us/About Our Students:** This is often a tab on the side of the page, or at the top, in the navigational header. It can also be located in a section called "For Prospective Students," or at the very bottom of the page, next to "Contact Us."

- **Strategic Plan:** This is usually in a section devoted to enrollment, or to future or prospective students. If the college does post a strategic plan, skim it; it'll give you a great idea about where it puts its resources, money, and energy.

- **Freshman Class Profile:** Colleges choose what information to put in their freshman class profile, and not all schools have it on their site. They also put it in different places. Using a Google site search (type "freshman class profile" into the search box in a college website) is probably the most efficient way to find it. The things a college will include, and the order in which they're placed on the profile, will tell you *exactly* what's important to that college. This may also contain information about aid dollars, GPA, and test scores, and demographic information for the most recent freshman class. Or use College Navigator or the College Board sites.

- **Why This College? (on the Admissions page):** When a college pitches themselves to you, they are telling you what their community is, and what it values. Colleges that focus on their outdoors programs are outdoorsy; colleges that focus on their math competitions are math-oriented. Colleges that highlight the political action of their students are politically oriented. Colleges that highlight the volunteer activities of their students love service; colleges that say they are

affiliated with a religious organization value that organization above all others. Although they rarely come
right out and say, "Here are our buzzwords," it's not
that complex to define. Don't think about it too hard;
just try to define what you're looking at.

Here are some of the buzzwords, or strategic priorities, we've
commonly used when building a "strategic profile," or mission
statement, for a college. They're certainly not the only buzzwords
out there, but hopefully they'll give you a feel for how schools often
define their students.

- Academically able/scholars/intellectual.
- Service.
- Spirituality.
- Green/sustainability.
- Global.
- Diverse (this can include racial and geographic
  diversity).
- Career-oriented.
- Entrepreneurship.
- Business experience.
- Community/family.
- Wellness/fitness.
- Technologically savvy.
- Character/ethics/morality.
- Outdoorsy (vs. indoorsy).
- Legacy/alumni.
- Math/science.
- Creative/performing arts.
- Politically aware.
- Socially active/oriented.

Go back to the list of your extracurriculars and interests. Can
you fit any of our buzzwords in the "Buzzwords" column?

Take a look at our example of Susie Senior's profile:

Category	Description	Buzzwords	Points
Leadership Experiences	Led a canoeing trip in the Boundary Waters	Outdoorsy, Fitness	5
	President of my High School Secular Humanist's Society	Community, Spirituality	5
	Led a team of my peers in a 5K charity run	Socially Active, Service, Fitness	4
	Organized the Spring Fling	Socially Active, Creative	3
	Helped bus elderly people to a local election	Service, Socially Active, Politically Aware	3
Activities: Sports, Clubs, Performing Arts	Member of the Snowboarding Club	Fitness, Outdoorsy	2
	Member of the Golf Team	Fitness, Outdoorsy	3
	Member of "Students for a Better World" recycling program	Socially Active, Green	3
	Member of Mock Trial	Career-oriented	4
	Member of GSA or GBLT	Diverse, Socially Active	3
	Mathlete, 2 years	Math, Scholar	4
	Write a style blog that documents my high school classmates	Socially Active, Technologically Savvy	5
Honors and Awards, Recognitions	Class President	Career-Oriented, Politically Active, Socially Active	5

	2nd place, State Science Fair	Science, Scholar	5
	3rd place, Regional Track and Field Championships, Javelin	Fitness	5
	Recipient of $400 Arts Grant from my town	Creative	5
Community Involvement, Service, Volunteer Work	Volunteered at a local Children's Hospital, read to inpatients	Service	4
	Play bridge with my grandmother and her friends twice a month	Service, Socially Active	3
Paid Work	Sandwich delivery, after school, 15 hours per week	Business Experience	3
	Sell my handmade jewelry at art fairs 4 times per year	Entrepreneurship, Creative	5

As you can see, Susie Senior has got a *lot* going on, and there's a fair amount of consistency as to what she's interested in. Looking at Susie—a jewelry-making outdoorswoman who plays bridge, recycles, belongs to her school's Gay-Straight Alliance, is a secular humanist, and a member of Mock Trial—at what kind of college do you think she'd excel (and have a good chance of being funded)? Probably one that values the same things Susie does: creative, outdoorsy, socially and politically active students. Susie wouldn't be a good candidate for aid at, say, Oral Roberts, Bob Jones, or Brigham Young University, all religious colleges; she also wouldn't have a very good experience at any of those schools. Although many search engines online encourage students to define the kinds of colleges they'd like to go to by choosing basic demographic information—such as size, location, and cost—we think that focusing on the activities you most enjoyed in high school is the best way to determine what kind of school is a good fit for you.

After you've figured out your stats, your interests and extra-curriculars, and your buzzwords, you're almost home free. Fill out our last chart, the MAP (Merit Aid Profile), to sum it all up.

In the "Me" row, you'll put your stats—your GPA, your SAT, and your ACT—and the buzzwords that you've pulled from your interests and extracurriculars. Put as many as you'd like.

If you don't have any colleges in mind, move ahead to the next chapter, and leave the remainder of the chart blank. If you already started searching, go on and complete the chart.

In the College A–O rows, you'll put the stats for the top 25 percent of the freshman class at however many colleges that you're interested in (go to page 147 to learn how to find the top 25 percent), along with buzzwords that you can find on the school's website. Ideally, you'll have at least two or three of the same buzzwords; if not, you'll want to make sure that your stats put you solidly in the top 20 to 25 percent.

If your stats are higher than the colleges, and you've got some similar buzzwords, go ahead and put a **Y** (for yes) in the "Chance of Funding" column. If your buzzwords don't match, you can still put a **Y**, but go back and look at the school's site. Could you really see yourself there? If your stats *and* buzzwords don't match, put an **N** (for no). If you mark any **N**s on this chart, don't bother applying to those schools—unless your EFC qualifies you for Pell. In that case, you may be able to get enough in need-based aid to make it affordable.

The MAP (Merit Aid Profile)

	GPA	SAT	ACT	Buzzwords	Chance of Funding?
Me					
College A					
College B					
College C					
College D					
College E					
College F					
College G					
College H					
College I					
College J					
College K					
College L					
College M					
College N					
College O					

Please bear in mind as you fill this out that it's certainly still possible to apply, be accepted, and get some aid at colleges where you're not in the top 25 percent. But applying can mean falling in love, and falling in love means taking on extra debt. Our MAP is essentially the simplest and most conservative method we would use with any student who needed to find a scholarship, and if you're in the middle 50 percent at most colleges, you will still get *some* aid. It simply may not be *enough* aid. The best bet you can make on a scholarship is to be in the top quartile of applicants. It's that simple.

The Cost-Based
College Search

To BE BLUNT, the absolute cheapest option for a college education is to attend a local community college for two years, and then transfer to another school. That allows you to get all of your prerequisites and core requirements out of the way, at an exceptionally reasonable price. The average annual tuition cost for a community college, according to the College Board, is $3,440. It also allows you to raise your grades substantially, if you need to—making you eligible for admission and merit aid to colleges that you may not otherwise be able to consider. If you are absolutely committed, you can earn this amount by putting away the earnings for about nine hours per week, 52 weeks per year, at $10 an hour. Double that for spending money or to give your folks some cash toward groceries or pay for your gas and car insurance.

However, there's a fair amount of missed opportunity cost here, and not all colleges accept transfer students or all of their credits. And the relationships that you'll develop with your peers and the faculty during the first two years of college are important. It can be difficult to transition into a new environment, when everyone around you has already had two years to make that school their own. There is, too, the compulsion to *get out of your parent's house.* You're 18 and ready to go. So why wait?

The traditional college search focuses primarily on brand ranking, as determined by ratings boards such as *U.S. News & World Report*, *The Princeton Review*, and *Forbes.* You would take your transcript into your high school guidance office, and the college counselor on hand will find the most competitive school you could gain admission to—the lowest possible threshold that your grades could overcome. Then you apply, and wait for acceptance, without considering cost as a factor. Many students simply apply to the most competitive schools they could conceivably gain admission to and pray for a scholarship, without understanding that if they're not in the top quartile of applicants, they likely won't receive enough aid to make it affordable.

Although we've covered it multiple times, if this is the first chapter you've taken a look at, we need you to understand something: The old paradigm of a "safety" and "reach" school is ridiculous. Throw it out the window. You should consider colleges the same way that many people consider graduate school: *It's about being funded.* There's no shame in being one of the best in the class, and there's so much diversity among the more than 4,400 colleges and universities in the United States—many of whom have incredibly devoted and highly educated faculty members— that you'll surely be able to find an environment you can excel in, and where you won't be overloaded with debt, whether it's a "top 50" school or not.

In Chapters 3, 4, 5, and 6, we covered how you're going to define the three most important elements of your college search: how much you can afford to pay outright, how much debt you're willing to take on, and what kind of a student you are. At the end of Chapter 6, we showed you our Merit Aid Profile, or MAP. You may have filled it out only with your stats, but as you begin searching for schools, you can add their information in and begin the process of separating the funded schools from the unfunded ones.

The MAP is an incredibly useful tool for two reasons: It allows you to define how your values align with a college, and whether or not you'll be in the top 25 percent. But if your family is in serious financial straits, and you can't meet anything even close to your EFC, we have a different chart for you to try later in this chapter. That means doing a college search that focuses almost exclusively on cost, using net price, your actual EFC, and your stats.

The cost-conscious search

If you're ready to move on with your life and get out of the house (or the idea of a community college doesn't appeal to you in any way), the next least expensive option is to go to a college in your home state, or in a neighboring state. That throws travel costs out the window—easily an extra $1,500 to $2,500 per year. You shouldn't have a car—that's just another waste of money—but you can bus, train, or carpool with the most ease from a college located in your home or neighboring state.

To begin the cost-conscious search, we recommend looking at colleges within a 250-mile radius of your hometown. Grab your laptop, a pen, and a piece of scratch paper, and go online.

Log on to nces.ed.gov/collegenavigator. You can use the search box in the left rail to get a list of all the colleges—public, private, or both—in your home and neighboring states. If you use the "map" function instead of the drop-down menu, you can select multiple states with ease. After you hit "Show Results," you'll get a hyper-linked list of colleges, where you can see sticker price, graduation rates, average student loan burden, and aid dollars awarded. It's not the sexiest or most sophisticated site, but the data is sound, and it's certainly the most reputable and reliable source of admission and financial aid information out there.

You can do the same thing at the College Board's admittedly more attractive website, bigfuture.collegeboard.org, although the College Board gives you more selection criteria—not all of which is a useful filter. Their aid filters, for example, don't appear to work very well, because not all colleges report that data to the College Board, but you can use their "College Search" to find colleges where you'll exceed (that is, be in the top 25 percent) admission requirements. Just enter your test scores into the "Admission" portion of the app. You'll create an account with them, but that's okay. They'll send you information throughout the duration of your search.

Using the Admission tool on the College Board "College Search" is incredibly useful for one reason: You can choose to see only colleges that are not-for-profit colleges. College Navigator also allows you to filter out for-profit colleges.

However, we do recommend that you *first* use College Navigator, and then follow with bigfuture.collegeboard.org. The reason is that College Navigator consistently lists net price, and bigfuture.college board.org does not.

Once you're looking at a list of all the colleges in your region, we recommend that you write down each school you're familiar with or interested in learning more about. Then head to the college's own website, and *read, read, read*! The college's own site is the best sources of information about majors, programs, student life, and the campus and town.

All colleges and universities are required by the federal government to display a net price calculator. However, that calculator is only required to display your eligibility for grant aid, based on averages by EFC bands; this means you may not get an accurate reading. These calculators will estimate your federal loans and grants the exact same way that FAFSA4caster does. Some colleges and universities may provide more sophisticated tools that show eligibility for merit- and need-based grants, but most will probably not. The most consistent and accurate information about net price will probably always come from College Navigator.

After you've paged through some college websites—try to look at 10 or so—head back to College Navigator, and type the colleges names into the search box. Pull up their individual profiles, and get out a pen.

What are you looking for at College Navigator?

What you're looking for at College Navigator are two things: the admission stats for each college, and the *net price* (located on each college's profile under a + Net Price tab, which allows you to expand the information available). The average net price is the average amount that full-time undergraduate students actually pay per year (after need- and merit-based aid is awarded). College Navigator divides up the averages by income for federal aid recipients, allowing you to view the specific average for the range of your family's household income. Net price is the best indication of what you would actually pay as a student in the middle 50 percent of applicants; if your stats put you above the middle 50 percent, you will likely receive more in aid, and a lower net price.

Use the Cost Conscious Search chart on page 169. Enter your stats and your Actual EFC (what you calculated in Chapters 4 and 5), and then add in the net price for your household's income range and the stats for the top 25 percent for each college.

As we discussed in the previous chapter, you'll get the highest possible amount of aid at most schools if you're in the top 25 percent of applicants or above, because need-based and merit aid dollars are generally awarded sequentially (the top 5 percent, then the top 10 percent, then the top 15 percent, and so on). In that chapter, we used data taken from the College Board, because it's the most commonly used site and it consistently showcases GPA. You can also use Peterson's. For test scores, it's fairly simple: You'll want to have test scores that are above the 75th percentile (which you can easily see, on the +Admission tab, at College Navigator). But GPA is a little trickier.

How will you know what the top 25 percent of the class is?

To find information about the top 25 percent of the class, you'll want to understand GPA as well as test scores. College Navigator does *not* report GPA, so you'll have to use the College Board. Go to collegeboard.org, type in the college's name, and on the profile, click "How Do I Stack Up?" You'll see a set of charts; most of the information that gets reported is the middle 50 percent—between the 25th and 75th percentile. Test scores are the simplest. So for a college that reports a middle 50 percent of SAT scores as 900–1250, the top 25 percent of the class has a 1250 or above; for ACT scores, for a college that reports the middle 50 percent of ACT as 25–29, the top 25 percent of the class has a 29 or above. Remember to convert old SAT scores from tests prior to March 2016 at collegereadiness .collegeboard.org.

GPA is sometimes difficult, because the division doesn't always add up. GPA is reported as a spread—and it's not always even. For Gonzaga, which we mentioned in Chapter 6, 47 percent of the class had a 3.75 GPA or above. Although it doesn't *always* align exactly, we can guesstimate by subtracting 3.75 from 4, dividing the remainder (.25) in half, then adding it to the reported GPA— determining that the top 25 percent had a GPA of around 3.875 (3.75 plus .125, or half of .25) or above.

Do you want a short cut? Go to bigfuture.collegeboard.org /college-search. Follow the instructions to place your data on college credential charts.

Other examples of GPA guesstimates, using the College Board's data

- At Goucher College in Maryland, 14 percent had a 3.75 GPA or above, and 12 percent had a GPA of 3.5 or above. This is perfectly simple math—14 + 12 = 26 percent. So to be in the top quartile, you'll need to have a GPA of 3.5 or above.
- At The College of Wooster in Ohio, 41 percent had a GPA of 3.75 or above. We'd wager that the top 25 percent had a GPA of 3.89 or above; we found that by dividing .25 by 41 (to discover the remaining percentage points), and multiplying the answer—roughly .006—by 24 (the difference between 41 and 25), to get .14. We added that .14 to 3.75 and got 3.89.

- At Eckerd College in Florida, 14 percent had a GPA of 3.75 or higher, and 17 percent had a GPA of 3.5 or above—meaning that the top 30 percent had a GPA of 3.5 or above, and the 25th percentile would fall somewhere between 3.5 and 3.75. We'd guesstimate that the top 25 percent of the class has at least a GPA of 3.62 or higher. We got to that number by dividing .25 (the difference between 3.5 and 3.75) by 17 (the number of percentage points in between), and then multiplying the answer, roughly .014, by 5 (the number of percentage points we need to subtract from our gross to get the 25 percent).

- Again, in the following chart, you'll enter your stats and your actual EFC (what you calculated in Chapters 4 and 5). Your stats will only go in the first row, but your actual EFC will go in every row.

- For each college, you'll add in the net price for your household's income range from the school's College Navigator profile, and the stats for the top 25 percent for each college, which you've calculated from the College Board's website.

- After you've entered all that information, you can determine whether or not your scores are equal to or higher than the stats you've entered for each college. If they are, add a **Y** (for yes) in the "Chance of Funding" column. If not, add an **N** (for no) in the Chance of Funding Column.

- Then, you'll subtract your Actual EFC (the amount your family can afford to pay out of pocket) from the college's net price (use the Net Price for your family's income range). That will calculate the Gap, or the amount of money you might need to receive above and beyond average aid. The Gap directly correlates to your chances of funding. If you've marked an **N** (for no) in the Chance of Funding column, and the Gap is a fairly substantial amount of money (a few thousand dollars or more), then mark **N** in the "Worth Applying" Column. But if there's no Gap, or you've marked a **Y** (for yes) in the Chance of Funding column, then go ahead and mark a **Y** in the "Worth Applying" column, and request an application!

If you're interested in schools outside of your home region, by all means, apply them to this chart—but remember that you'll need additional funding for travel costs. How should you search for colleges outside your home region? Well, if you're interested in a certain state, search College Navigator or the College Board by state; if you're interested in a certain major or program, use those criteria. We also recommend that you talk to your high school guidance counselor, and make it abundantly clear that you're in need of a scholarship, and you'd only like to apply to places where you're in the top 25 percent of applicants. Specify a program and your interests, and the counselor should be able to help you make a list.

Wherever you've marked a **Y** in the Worth Applying column, go online to that college's website and request an application. But before you send in your application—and your nonrefundable application fee—you might want to visit the school. For more information about how you can use the campus visit to connect with the financial aid office, read on to Chapter 8.

What's the Gap? The cost-conscious search

	GPA	SAT	ACT	Chance of Funding?	Net Price	Actual EFC	The Gap: Net Price-EFC	Worth Applying?
Me								
College A								
College B								
College C								
College D								
College E								
College F								
College G								
College H								
College I								
College J								
College K								
College L								
College M								
College N								
College O								

8

Everything You Need to Know Before You Hand in Your Paperwork

BEFORE YOU SEND in your applications, you'll need to know exactly what documentation each school requires, and when.

After you've used either our MAP or Cost-Conscious Search charts, or both, you should have an excellent idea of where you'd like to apply. If you can establish a relationship with the financial aid office at this point in the process, before you even submit an application, that relationship could really work to your advantage. Not only does contacting the aid office demonstrate a commitment to the school and a serious level of maturity, but it allows the financial aid administrators (FAAs) to remember your name and get to know you. FAAs can't advocate as effectively for students they don't know, and although every officer tries to be fair, it's always helpful to make a personal connection. In some cases, that isn't possible, but either way, you'll want to know and understand all the protocols that each school has in place for its financial aid dollars before you spend hours of your time on an application.

The first step is to thoroughly mine the website for any and all information. Here's what you're looking for; if you can't find it on the site, make a note of it for later.

You want to know:

- Does it require the FAFSA only, or is the CSS PROFILE required also?
- Does it require an institutional financial aid application?
- What, if any, specific merit aid scholarships does it offer? What are the requirements for eligibility?
- Do merit scholarships require a special application? Is there an on-campus competition, or an application deadline for consideration?
- Does it publish a matrix or chart defining who gets what kind of merit award?
- Does it assign financial aid officers or counselors to prospective students?
- If not, do all aid questions get routed through the admission office?
- Who is the appropriate person to contact for more information?

You'll want to introduce yourself to the right person from the start; you don't want to be a thorn in someone else's side. If you can't determine who the appropriate contact is, send the following email to the admission office (usually admission(s)@college.edu; look on the "Contact Us" page for prospective students to find out).

Dear Admission Office,

I'm a prospective student for the fall of [the year you would be a freshman]. I'll be applying for financial aid, and I'd like to make sure that I have all the right information at hand. Who should I contact with my questions about this? I'm happy to communicate by phone or by email.

Thanks so much for your assistance; my contact information is below.

Best,

[Your name, email address, and phone number]

Once you've discovered who the appropriate contact is, send the following email:

Dear [Person],

I'm a prospective student for the fall of [the year you would be a freshman]. I'm very, very interested in the possibility of attending [College X], but I will need to apply for financial aid. I've read all the information on your website about the process for applying for need- and merit-based aid, but I was wondering if you would be able to answer the following questions for me:

[insert questions not covered by the website here]

Additionally, do you have any other advice for navigating the admission and scholarship process? I've estimated my EFC at [whatever you estimated using—NPC, FAFSA4caster], but my family is only able to afford [your actual EFC, which you discussed with your family in Chapters 4 and 5], and I would like to keep my loans to a minimum. I'm a resident of [your state]. Do you have any advice for someone in my situation—specific scholarships or grants that I may not have heard of? My combined SAT critical reading and math score is [your score]; my ACT composite score is [your score]; my GPA is [your GPA].

Thank you very much for your time and assistance. If you have time for a phone conversation, my contact info is listed below.

Best,

[Your name, your year in high school, your high school, and your phone number].

It's possible that the person you're communicating with won't be able to tell you anything that you can't learn online. But you never know; the college in question may have scholarships that aren't advertised or published online; the officer in question might have gone to your high school, or sympathize with your situation. It is always, always worth asking, and you don't lose anything at all by emailing.

Even if he or she is not terribly helpful, keep this person's name and contact information, and be polite and grateful. No matter how unhelpful he or she is, be sure to respond with a thank-you email. When you visit, he or she should be one of the first people you check in with and say hello to.

If your finances are really, really tight, we don't recommend visiting a college until you've been accepted. Visiting can be costly, but more importantly, visiting is romance; it's the equivalent of going on a date with flowers, candy, a concert, and a hayride under the moon in the dark. Colleges pull out all the stops for prospective students (known in many places as "prospys"), and if you haven't been admitted or you don't receive enough aid to make it affordable, you could be tempted to take out more student loans than you should. However, we love college fairs! They're usually in your hometown or the nearest big city, and it's a great opportunity to connect with the admission office and get all your questions answered. Best of all, they're free. Go to nacacnet.org for more information about locations and dates for a college fair near you. You can also make contact with individual admission counselors when they visit your school; for more information about who is visiting and when, see your high school guidance counselor.

Once you've had your questions answered for each school you're planning on applying to, you'll need to actually send in applications. Skip ahead to the next chapter to learn how to optimize your application for scholarships and merit aid.

After you've sent off your applications, you'll need to finally fill out and submit your financial aid paperwork. The next section tells you what you need to know.

Filling out the FAFSA

You can submit the FAFSA on or after October 1 of the year before you intend to enroll. If you will be graduating from high school in June 2018 and starting college that fall, you can file the FAFSA any time after October 1, 2017. You can fill it out online, at fafsa.gov. You can also submit a paper application, printable from the FAFSA website, which will take longer to process, but both electronic and paper versions are free. The custodial parent is required to fill out the FAFSA. For an understanding of terms used on the FAFSA and how it breaks down, read Chapter 2.

Required documents to have on-hand to complete the FAFSA

For both parents *and* students:

- Social Security numbers (SSNs).
- Dates of birth.
- W2, tax return 1040 or 1040 A or 1040 EZ. This includes the stepparent married to the custodial parent.
- Record of child support to children of another household.
- Housing, food, and other living allowances, such as military, clergy, and others (including cash payments and cash value of benefits).
- Veterans' non-education benefits, including disability, death pension, or dependency and indemnity compensation (DIC), or VA educational works-study allowances.
- Any record of other untaxed income not reported, such as worker's compensation or disability.
- Current total balance as of today of cash, savings, and checking accounts.
- Current net worth and investments, real estate, Coverdell, and 529 plans.

- Net worth of any current business or investment farm. This does not include a small business of which the parents control more than 50 percent and has 100 or fewer full time employees, and does not include the value of a family farm that the student and/or parent lives on and operates.
- Student records of unreported untaxed income.
- Net worth of current business or investment farms.
- Students who are eligible non-citizens only will need to provide their A number, which can be found on their alien registration card (also known as their green card).

If any of those don't apply to you or your parents (like veterans' benefits), disregard them.

You may find it helpful to use the "FAFSA on the Web" worksheet, which you can download from fafsa.ed.gov, to organize and complete the questions on paper before entering online. The questions are listed in the same order that they appear in FAFSA on the web.

Filling out the CSS PROFILE

The CSS PROFILE is similar to the FAFSA, although it's more detailed and it's not free. Both the custodial and non-custodial parent must fill out and submit the PROFILE, which can be found online at profile online.collegeboard.com. The initial fee is $25 to submit the form to one school, and $16 for each additional school report.

What you need to have on-hand to complete the CSS PROFILE

Student *and* both sets of parents:

- Social Security numbers (SSNs).
- Dates of birth.
- Federal income tax returns 1040s and W2s (two most recent years), and any other records of money earned in the most recent years.

- Record of untaxed income and benefits for the last two years.
- Current bank statements.
- Current mortgage information.
- Records of savings, stocks, bonds, trusts, and other investments.
- Temporary Assistance for Needy Families (TANF) or Supplemental Security Income (SSI).
- If either parent is unemployed, you'll need the date that unemployment began.
- Civil service or union retirement plan.
- Current value of tax deferred retirement, pension, annuity, and savings plans including IRA, SRA, Keogh, SEP, 401K, 403B, 408, 457, and 501C.
- Parent earning projection for current tax year.
- Current market value of home, value of mortgage, year purchased, original purchase price, and the same information on any other real estate owned by parents.
- For a business owned and operated by either parent, you'll need the following: the original start date, total current market value, amount owed on business, number of employees, who owns and percentage of ownership, other family members with ownership and their percentage of ownership, and other family members who receive salary (names, relationship, yearly salary, or wages).
- For a farm owned and operated by either parent, you'll need the following: the name of your farm, number of acres, current market value per acre, current total market value, amount owed, and location with address.
- Parent child support paid to another household.
- Parent educational loan repayment, and amount paid in current and previous tax years—on their own

educational loans (does not include parent PLUS loan for child).

- Amount of medical and dental expenses not covered by insurance or a medical or dental plan.
- Total elementary, junior high, and high school tuition paid in prior and current year, and how many children you paid for and expect to pay for.
- Monthly home mortgage payment.
- For a non-custodial parent for current and previous years, an agreement of how much the non-custodial parent will pay for college.
- VA benefits earned/expect to earn.
- Student tuition benefits from parent employer or student employer.
- Student uniform gift to minor (value of account).
- Parents report for all other children (report of all dependent family members except this student and parents):
  - Where they go to school.
  - Associated fees or tuition, scholarship or grants, and dollar amounts for the next two years.
  - Whether they will be enrolled in high school or college the following year.
- Year, make, and model of motor vehicles.
- Additional real estate: year of purchase, purchase price, current value, and amount owed.
- Schedule C businesses: name, amount invested, and percentage of ownership.
- If either parent is the beneficiary of a trust or estate: type of trust, value, terms, and other pertinent information (if parent has received).
- If another family member is a beneficiary of a trust: type of trust, value, terms, and other pertinent information.
- Credit card information to pay the fee for the PROFILE ($25 application fee, $16 per institution sent).

Additional documents that may be requested by colleges

Signed copies of the federal tax return for the student, the parent, or both are frequently requested by colleges as are copies of W2s, even if the student's FAFSA has been approved without being submitted for verification.

A tax transcript may be requested—it is free from the IRS and can be ordered online at irs.gov. You may receive a copy electronically or through the U.S. mail service.

Verification happens when the college in question confirms the data reported on your FAFSA. Your school has the authority to contact you for documentation that supports income and other information that you reported. Colleges have the right to withhold financial aid offers until requested documentation is received. Be careful when you fill out the FAFSA: Students are selected for verification when there is mismatched information. If your SSN is incorrect or missing for either the student or the parent, names don't match, the number of people in the household doesn't look right, or any calculations are not reasonable, you will be selected for verification. Colleges are required to verify the information on all students selected as a result of the federal processing system and on students for whom the college determines there is a conflict of information in the data provided. Colleges must also write and follow a policy for the selection of additional students for verification in compliance with current federal regulations.

Special circumstances

Documentation must be provided for specific expenses not listed in the FAFSA or Profile that occurred since filing or not listed at all. As an example, supporting an elderly relative's nursing home expenses, recent parent job loss, or a disabled child all qualify as "special circumstances." Colleges may require copies of payment made to a nursing home or care center, or a letter of termination of employment. In other words, you need to prove it happened.

Non-custodial parent waiver

For colleges that require the non-custodial PROFILE, and the non-custodial parent refuses to comply or can't be found, then the college will likely require documentation. Institutions may supply a Request for Waiver of Non-Custodial Parent Information form that outlines the acceptable documentation, or they may simply request specific documents, such as evidence of non-payment of child support. A letter of support from an individual with knowledge of the family situation may be required, such as a counselor, minister, or officer of the court.

Selective Service registration

All males aged 18, who are U.S. citizens, *must* register with the Selective Service. The federal government will conduct a database check when you file the FAFSA. Men may register on the FAFSA if they complete it online. If the student is exempt from registering for the Selective Service, a copy of the Status Information Letter may be required.

Further understanding financial aid policies

Summer earnings

If you are applying for financial aid, many colleges will expect that you, the student, will earn money during the summer to use for school. It may or may not say so on the website, but it may be listed as a resource on your financial aid award, when it's ultimately sent to you. If you can't have a job or take paid work in the summer for any reason, discuss it with your financial aid officer. Although it isn't likely that he or she will let you off the hook for summer earnings, it doesn't hurt to ask.

Outside scholarships

Outside scholarships, also known as *private* scholarships, can come from anywhere that *isn't* the college itself, or the state or federal government. They can come from corporations, from fellowship organizations, and from community or religious institutions. Your college may adjust your financial aid as a result of your receiving outside scholarships.

- *If your college met your full need*, meaning that the combination of your EFC and your financial aid package *equals* the total cost of attendance, *and* you have federal grants or work-study, then you generally can't have more financial aid than the cost of attendance. This is known as an "over award," and the college will likely reduce your financial aid package. But don't worry; they'll begin by reducing your loans and/or work-study. If that's still not sufficient (because you have some amazing, enormous scholarship), only *then* will they reduce the amount of their money (institutional dollars) that you're receiving. But not all schools do this; some schools might try to replace their money *first*. If this is the case, lobby to have them reduce your loan or work-study first; begin by sending an email, then call the officer in question as a last step.
- *If you are receiving only merit aid (not need-based aid), your college should have a published policy for outside scholarships on its website.* What you want is for the college to "stack" the outside scholarship on *top* of your merit aid from the college itself, so that you can get the full amount of both. Not all colleges will do this, however. You can try to lobby for scholarship stacking, but you will probably not be successful, if the published policy states otherwise. If any other school to which you've been admitted with an equal offer

(against the cost of attendance) agrees to stack the outside scholarship, make sure you get it in writing—then use that document in an appeal to keep the full amount of your outside scholarship at your first-choice school.

Satisfactory academic progress

The federal government will expect you to make regular progress toward receiving your degree. The school's course catalog (updated each semester or annually) will inform you of those requirements.

Merit aid renewal policy

Many colleges have minimum GPA requirements for scholarship renewal from year to year. They're typically listed on the letter offering you the aid. Know what the requirements are, and keep up that GPA.

School-specific policies for payments, interest charged, withdrawal from courses, and refunds

These policies, which are different at each college, will be listed on the individual websites and in the course catalogs. If you don't follow the policies, the fees can stack up and prevent you from enrolling in your courses or even graduating on time. Parents, put the required dates on a calendar each semester, and give a copy to your child.

The financial aid timeline

We've put together a timeline of every single thing you could possibly do during the college admission process, from the spring of your sophomore year of high school to the day you enroll in college. You don't have to do all of it, but you should do most of it. Rip it out of the book, or print it out from our website, and tape it to your refrigerator or desk. Check things off, cross them out in red pen, or even use Wite-Out so that your tasks slowly disappear from the page—whatever you need to do!

Timeline	For Parents	For Students	What Chapter?
September– October, Junior Year	Complete FAFSA4caster, at Fafsa4caster.ed.gov. Have a candid discussion with your spouse or former spouse about paying for college. Start making a plan to modify your budget.	Take PSAT. Meet with high school counselor. Attend a college fair.	1, 2, 5
November– January, Junior Year	Have a family discussion about your Actual EFC.	Have a family discussion about paying for college. Start saving, get a part-time job, stash money away for college expenses. Get rid of your car?	3, 4, 5
January– March, Junior Year	Help your child search for schools, and help him or her fill out our MAP and Cost-Conscious Search charts.	Search for colleges. Complete our MAP and/or Cost-Conscious Search charts.	6, 7
April– May, Junior Year	Revisit your conversation about paying for college. Are you on track? Have you had any major changes in your financial position? Look at the net prices you calculated using our Cost-Conscious Search chart in Chapter 7. Can you still afford that?	Take SAT and/or ACT.	
June– August, Summer Before Senior Year	Do some local college visits, if possible. (We recommend that you save your money and don't go on expensive visits until your child is admitted.)	Sign up for FASTWEB.	9

September, Senior Year	Put important dates on your calendar.	Take SAT and/or ACT again, or take an SAT/ACT prep course. Build a calendar of admission and scholarship deadlines.	6, 7, 9
October, Senior Year	File the FAFSA. Make sure your child is organizing his or her admission materials correctly.	File the FAFSA. Make sure you list the codes of all schools on your list. (You may list up to 10.) Attend college fairs. Use the MAP and Cost-Conscious Search charts again to narrow down your choices. Request applications, and fill them out. Update your deadline calendar.	2, 6, 7, 9
November, Senior Year	File PROFILE for Early Decision Profile schools. Read your child's essays and review his or her applications for accuracy. Send all materials U.S. mail, receipt requested to prove your child has met deadlines, if you're not using electronic applications.	File CSS PROFILE for Early Decision PROFILE schools. Retake the SAT and/or ACT. Fill out applications for admission. Check your deadline calendar. Keep copies of everything you send.	2, 8
December, Senior Year	Watch for admission and scholarship offers; many scholarship offers are sent immediately following admission.	Watch for admission and scholarship offers; many schools send them electronically via email or through a portal in their website.	10

January, Senior Year	File federal taxes	File federal taxes.	2, 8
		Complete scholarship competitions (applications and essays and referrals if necessary).	
		Go to scholarship events/interviews at your colleges.	
February, Senior Year	Many colleges send financial aid packages to students online. Use the charts in Chapter 10 to track your child's offers.	Watch your email for your admission letter and financial aid package. Use the charts in Chapter 10 to track your offers.	2, 8, 10
March, Senior Year	File your FAFSA immediately (many state deadlines are March 1).	File your FAFSA immediately (many state deadlines are March 1).	2, 8, 10
	Immediately meet any requests for subsequent information for financial documentation.	Meet any requests for subsequent information for financial aid.	
		Use the charts in Chapter 10 to track your offers.	
April, Senior Year	Go to admitted student events and/or a private campus visit.	Go to admitted student events and/or a private campus visit.	10
	Meet with financial aid officers to discuss the financial aid award.	Meet with financial aid officers to discuss the financial aid award.	
	An enrollment deposit is due May 1.		

May, Senior Year	Your enrollment deposit is due May 1. Find out the payment options for your child's school. (Many first payments are due in June.) Construct a plan to pay your share in full. Know where your money is coming from. Deposits may be refundable until May 1, so pay early to get priority for housing and registration, so if that is offered by your child's first-choice school.	Your enrollment deposit is due May 1. Don't miss the deadline. Many schools withdraw offers of admission in May when their classes are full. Go outside. Stop thinking about college.	
June, Senior Year	Pick dates for summer orientation, if possible.	Sign up for summer orientation, if possible.	
July, Summer Before College	Apply for Parent PLUS loan. Get your child's immunization records from your doctor. Read *Letting Go* by Karen Levin Coburn and Madge Lawrence Treeger.	Apply for Direct loan. Contact your roommate as soon as you get the name. Submit your immunization form.	2, 3
August, Summer Before College	Complete promissory notes. Have your child pay the bill. Take your child to college!	Complete promissory notes and electronic entrance counseling (required). Pay your bill. Enjoy move-in day, and get started!	

9

Merit Aid and the Application

BEFORE YOU CAN get any aid, you do have to be admitted. This chapter outlines the basic steps you need to take for an efficient and low-stress application process, and how to tailor your applications to ensure that you're an excellent candidate for any and all merit aid dollars available.

Now that you've narrowed it down to a list of schools at which you can get funded, either using our MAP in Chapter 6, our Cost-Conscious Search in Chapter 7, or both, you're ready to send out applications.

You may be thinking that you'd like to visit before you apply; we recommend that you wait to visit until after you've applied and been accepted. As we've said before, visiting can mean falling in love . . . and you're not ready to say, "I love you, College," just yet. Hold off on the declarations of forever and always until they've made you an offer of admission, and hopefully given you a financial aid award.

How many colleges should I apply to?

We recommend that you apply to seven schools or less; certainly no more than 10. Even if you're applying online, using the college's own forms, or the Common Application, applying to more than 10 schools is a waste of your time and money. If you've done your research, and you're in the top 25 to 50 percent of applicants, you'll likely be accepted. It's not a game of chance, so you don't need to apply to every college on earth. We recommend that you apply to only two or three schools at which you're only in the top 50 percent of applicants; you'll still get aid, but you may not get enough to make it affordable.

If your list is small, apply to at least three, if you can. We don't want you to leave all of your eggs in just one or two baskets, even if you're in the top 25 percent at each place.

There are several reasons why you should keep your applications between three and seven. The first, and most important, is for your own peace of mind. College applications are a fair amount of work, and each requires a different essay and supporting materials (even if they use the Common or Universal College Application). Each application should take you a few hours of effort or more. They'll also all have different deadlines and due dates. Don't you have enough to keep track of in your life? And really, if you're applying to more than 10 colleges, all you're doing is postponing the final decision. After all, you can only attend one.

Cost, too, is a factor. Many schools charge a processing fee when you're submitting paper applications instead of electronic ones, usually somewhere in the range of $25 to $75.

For colleges that require the CSS PROFILE, you'll pay a fee to the College Board of $25 for the first college, and $16 for each subsequent school. You'll need to submit your test scores to each school, which costs $12 per score for the fifth score and up for the SAT and ACT, and your school may charge you to send out transcripts.

Colleges cannot ask you to list or rank order *other* schools to which you are applying. If you encounter a question on an application requesting this, don't complete it.

Should I apply early decision?

Early decision is binding. That means that if a college accepts you, you've already agreed to enroll. Early decision is perfect for your number-one choice, but only if you're absolutely sure you can afford it. So if you've done all the research you can, and you know, without a doubt, that you're not only in the top 25 percent of the class, but your other credentials are aligned with the college's values, and you would go there in a heartbeat, then yes. Go ahead. But if you can't assure yourself of any or all of those things, then use an early notification deadline; that will signal to the college that you're serious about enrolling. *We recommend using early notification deadlines whenever possible, as long as they're not binding.*

How do I get started?

The absolute best way to begin is to make a paper calendar and a to-do list. You can certainly use Google Calendar as well, but we like paper calendars—you'll find that you internalize the information more easily once you write it down by hand. Mark down application deadlines for each college (again, using as many non-binding early notification deadlines as possible), dates to arrange sending your test scores and transcripts (spring semester, if possible), and dates to request recommendations. You can also use Google Calendar; if you have a smart phone, you can set Google Calendar to beep your phone and remind you of all of your deadlines.

You'll send your SAT and ACT scores online or when you register for the tests, and for your transcripts, you'll need to set up an appointment with your high school guidance counselor. If you take either test again, make sure you send those new scores (only if they're higher), no matter when you take the test. A higher score—even if it's sent in during your spring semester of your senior year—may allow the admission and financial aid office to increase your financial aid award.

How do colleges decide who gets in?

Admitting any student is essentially a five-step process, beginning with the simplest method of evaluation colleges have: your academic credentials. At each step, your application will move from one pile (or electronic folder) to the next. We cover the specifics later in this chapter, but we'd like to give you an outline of how we've admitted students in the past.

1. Academic credentials

Many colleges will recalculate your GPA, creating a core GPA of only academic subjects, and will give you a weighted advantage for AP and Honors courses. They'll also assess your SAT and ACT scores. This is the first hurdle, and hopefully, you've already assessed whether or not you can pass it with flying colors.

2. Talents, leadership, interests, and activities

Do you value what the college values? This ties back to the buzz-words we defined in Chapter 6. If you're an atheist who supports a woman's right to choose, for example, Bob Jones University will have absolutely no interest in you; conversely, Oberlin is less likely to be interested in an evangelical Christian who is a member of the NRA and junior supporter of the Tea Party. Openly gay or trans-gender peaceniks may be less comfortable at the Naval Academy or any other military school, and ROTC kids who love structure may not find a home at Hampshire College, where there are no grades. You get the idea. A college whose values and personal characteristics oppose your own may admit you, but it certainly won't waste a single dime encouraging you to attend.

3. Character and values

What do your references say about you? Are you a "good kid," or are you "one of the most sportsmanlike and gracious intramural athletes I've ever seen"? The more specific your recommendations are, the better. Recommendation letters are always positive—yours should highlight what's special about you, not just what's good.

4. Advocacy

If there are more qualified applicants than a college needs to fill the freshman class, the admission officers will have a committee meeting and discuss your case for admission (and/or aid). This is when your admission counselor can *really* help you. She or he will be your advocate, but they'll only support you as much as you allow. You've got to let your admission counselor get to know you! Respond to emails and answer phone calls; often, the counselor has the discretionary power to advocate for your admission and improve your merit aid by $1,000 to $2,000 or more.

5. Demonstrated interest in attending

Is it clear that this college is one you would absolutely attend? Admission officers can smell ambivalence a million miles away— and you make it easier when you write on your application that this school is a second, third, or even fourth choice for you. If there's a space for it, always tell them that [College X] is your number-one choice. If they give you the best financial aid offer, it will be. It's not a lie, it's a conditional truth.

———

As you can see from this process, although grades are the first hurdle to surpass, intent and fit play a very large role. If you haven't used our MAP in Chapter 6, go back and try to define the values of each school you're applying to. You'll need to remember those values for your application.

What goes on each application?

In order to make it past hurdle number 2 and hurdle number 3, you'll need to make sure that you've highlighted the right activities (and garnered the most appropriate recommendations) for each college. Use our MAP from Chapter 6 to define each school, then make a list for each college that connects their values with your specific extracurriculars. *When you list your activities, talents, interests, and extracurriculars on each application, make sure the activities that align best with the college's values are at the top of each section.* Order is a tricky thing; it signals rank, importance, and intent, without *technically* doing so. And admission officers are human, just like anyone else; they'll see an extracurricular at the top of a page, and assume it's either something you're incredibly passionate about, something you absolutely excelled in, or both.

Example: Susie Senior's applications

Remember Susie Senior from Chapter 6? Well, Susie, a resident of California, is applying to several different kinds of schools up and down the West Coast. She doesn't know what she'd like to major in, but she poked around, used some arithmetic for guesstimates, and created her MAP with the following colleges and the data she collected about their top 25 percent.

	GPA	SAT Verbal	SAT Math	ACT	Buzzwords	Chance of Funding?
Susie Senior	3.62	730	650	31		
Whittier	3.80	580	590	25	Creative, community, scholar, fitness	Y
Evergreen State College	3.5	640	590	26	Green/sustainability, outdoorsy, creative	Y
Lewis & Clark	3.9	710	680	30		N
Pomona	3.95	780	770	34		N
University of Puget Sound	3.8	680	680	32		N
UC Berkeley	3.95	710	760	33		N
Otis College of Art and Design	3.6	560	590	24	Creative, community, socially active	Y

Now, Susie has an absolutely amazing sheet of extracurriculars, but she's not at the top of her class. We're guessing that she's a lot like you—active, engaged, and smart. Susie is someone who is better at actively *doing* than taking tests and getting perfect grades. And if she'd like to apply to either Lewis & Clark, Puget Sound, or UC Berkeley, she *may* get enough in aid because of her spectacular extracurriculars—but her grades alone won't guarantee that, which is why she marked Ns for those colleges. Susie needs a guarantee; she absolutely needs a scholarship. And she doesn't stand a chance of getting merit aid at Pomona, although she could probably get admitted.

Susie defined those buzzwords by looking at those colleges' websites. She's going to make sure that on each of her applications to Whittier, Evergreen, and Otis, her activities line up with what they're looking for. Susie profiled herself and this chart is what she came up with.

Category	Description	Buzzwords	Points
Leadership Experiences	Led a canoeing trip in the Boundary Waters	Outdoorsy	5
	President of my high school Secular Humanist's Society	Community, Spirituality	5
	Led a team of my peers in a 5K charity run	Socially Active, Service	4
	Organized the Spring Fling	Socially Active, Creative	3
	Helped bus elderly people to a local election	Service, Socially Active, Politically Aware	3
Activities: Sports, Clubs, Performing Arts	Member of the snowboarding club	Fitness, Outdoorsy	2
	Member of the golf team	Fitness, Outdoorsy	3
	Member of "Students for a Better World" recycling program	Socially Active, Green	3
	Member of Mock Trial	Career-oriented	4
	Member of GSA or GBLT	Diverse	3
	Mathlete, two years	Math, Scholar	4

	Write a style blog that documents my high school classmates	Socially Active, Technologically Savvy	5
Honors and Awards, Recognitions	Class president	Career-Oriented, Politically Active, Socially Active	5
	2nd place, State Science Fair	Science, Scholar	5
	3rd place, Regional Track and Field Championships, javelin	Fitness	5
	Recipient of $400 arts grant from my town	Creative	5
Community Involvement, Service, Volunteer Work	Volunteered at a local children's hospital, read to inpatients	Service	4
	Play bridge with my grand-mother and her friends twice a month	Service, Socially Active	3
Paid Work	Sandwich delivery, after school, 15 hours per week	Business Experience	3
	Sell my handmade jewelry at art fairs four times per year	Entrepreneurship, Creative	5

For Whittier, a formerly Quaker but now secular college, which values creativity (its mascot is the Poets), community (its website stresses paired and team-taught coursework), scholars (its website emphasizes learning and engagement), and fitness (those Poets play a lot of sports), Susie's going to make sure that she lists the following experiences at the top of each category:

- President of her high school Secular Humanist's Society.
- Mathlete.
- State Science Fair.
- Regional Track and Fitness Championships.

- Arts grant recipient.
- Handmade jewelry sales.

Even though these aren't necessarily Susie's most stand-out experiences—Class President is certainly a very big deal—listing them first shows that Susie *valued and cared about those experiences the most*. Admission officers won't disregard what's listed underneath them; they will still take your entire resume into account. But Susie is sending a message to Whittier that she cares about what they care about—even if she wasn't always the "best."

For Evergreen State College, which values the outdoors, green/sustainability, and creativity, Susie will make sure the following experiences are at the top of each category:

- Canoeing trip in the Boundary Waters.
- "Students for a Better World" recycling program.
- Golf team.
- Snowboarding club.
- Arts grant recipient.
- Handmade jewelry sales.

And finally, for Otis College of Art and Design, an arts school that values creative, community-minded, and socially active students, she'll highlight:

- Arts grant recipient.
- Style blog.
- Class president.
- Handmade jewelry sales.
- President of her High School Secular Humanist's Society.
- Organized the Spring Fling.

You'll want to highlight the experiences and activities that make you the best possible match for each school. Try using a few colored pencils on your personal profile—Green for College A, Blue for College B, and so on—and circle the experiences that work best for each school.

Don't be afraid to really redefine your paid work experiences, as well. If you had an after school job, think about what kind of business it was (retail? service?), what you learned about their product, and how it altered or enhanced your own character. Paid work experiences are wonderful material for your personal statement, too.

You'll also want to tailor your recommendations for each school, if you can. For the activities that align most closely with each school, find out if you can get a recommendation from the faculty advisor or adult who led your group. What would Susie do? For Whittier, Susie would ask for recommendations from the faculty advisor for the Secular Humanist's society, and possibly the town official who oversaw her $400 arts grant, or the Mathlete coach. For Evergreen, Susie would focus on her group from the Boundary Waters; she could get a group letter from them, detailing her leadership, and ask either of her coaches from the golf team or snowboarding club to write not just about her athletic prowess, but her behavior as a teammate. For Otis, Susie would want to get an amazing letter from the town official who oversaw her $400 arts grant, any faculty advisor who oversaw her style blog, and the faculty advisor for the dance committee.

Working those two angles—highlighting the right experiences and tailoring your recommendations—are absolutely the best ways to ensure that your application gets considered for the best merit aid available. But when it comes to the application, there's always more. We'll keep it brief; there are dozens of books out there about how to write an outstanding application. But you've *got* to know the basics and what mistakes to avoid. Read on for our application basics, and skip to the end of the chapter if you're looking for ways to supplement your application, go the extra mile, or address slip-ups in an extra essay.

The perfect application: common mistakes and how to avoid them

The biggest mistakes that students make are really simple ones, and they usually fall into one of two categories: misspelling the name of the school, your own name, or anything else on the application; and *sending the wrong materials to the wrong school.* When Ruth was an admission counselor at Gustavus, she used to get about a dozen essays for St. Olaf annually because students put their essays in the wrong envelopes or attached them to the wrong electronic app. If you can't get the basics right, your admission counselor won't be able to advocate for you very effectively. Make sure that everything goes to the right place. We like to use color-coded sticky notes to make sure that we don't misplace anything.

For spelling, you've got to check, double-check, and check a third time. You're asking the admission officers not only to admit you to a competitive academic program, but to give you money as well. Don't give them any excuse to pass you over (or an opportunity to advocate for someone else). When it comes to grammar, you *must* have someone else read your work. We've all had times when the sentence at hand seemed clear as day to us, but completely muddled to someone else. We became sentence-blind, so to speak, and we couldn't see it. Watch out for misplaced modifiers and double entendres. Carol remembers a girl who wrote an essay about her volunteer work in Africa in which she proudly told us she "treated wounds in the bush"; this may be an acceptable colloquialism in Australia, but certainly not in the United States. Seemingly simple yes-and-no and either/or questions can also get easily confused. For example, if the application asks about sex instead of gender, the correct answer is "M" or "F," not, as we once saw, "only once, in Duluth."

Essays and short answers on your admission materials are *not* the right moments to try and expand your vocabulary. It is especially not the time to use archaic or obsolete terms just to demonstrate that you can a) use a thesaurus, and b) spell them correctly. If you volunteer every two weeks with Habitat for Humanity, say just that—don't say that you "go on a fortnightly basis." Or if you come from a big family, say that—don't go with capacious, colossal, or commodious. We're not saying that you should be casual, but you don't need to beat the admission office over the head with your club of $10 SAT words. It looks ridiculous, and more often than not, students display how *poorly* they understand language, instead of how well. You do not want to be the student whose essay or short answer is read aloud at lunch to provide some cheap laughs for the admission office (and yes, every admission officer does that now and again).

If you're sending in a paper application (which we don't recommend—there's almost always an additional fee, and most schools have free electronic apps), do not use glitter, stickers, colored markers, photo collages, or anything else that you wouldn't use when applying for a job. This will make your admission officer either want to throw your application in the trash, or simply refuse to advocate for you. No one likes a glitter bomb in a manila envelope, confetti, or scratch-and-sniff stickers. No smiley faces or doodling in the margins; no calligraphy or cursive. Use pencil, have someone double- and triple-check for accuracy, then rewrite in blue or black pen, and write clearly, in print.

The personal statement and/or the essay

Remember that, just as you did with your extracurriculars and activities, you should tailor your personal statement to each school. Let's take a look at what Susie Senior would do:

- For Whittier, Susie would focus on her scholarly achievements—perhaps what it's really like to be a girl in the Mathletes, or how Secular Humanism reflects longstanding religious tenets from all cultures (just without God).
- For Evergreen State College, Susie would focus on her commitment to the outdoors, starting perhaps with an anecdote from her canoeing trip, or her recycling club.
- For Otis, Susie would highlight her most creative pursuits, and how she's brought them to the public sphere. That could draw from her experience applying for her arts grant, from selling her jewelry, or even decorating the Spring Fling dance.

No matter what you end up focusing on for your statement or personal essay, you'll want to capture the reader's attention, and maybe even allow him or her to feel the emotion of the moment. The most powerful essay Ruth ever read, for example, came to Agnes Scott College from a young woman who wrote about her family's escape from Thailand. They fled in the middle of the night, and she described each detail of the journey: hurrying along the streets toward the shore, getting into a tiny boat and floating for days until a larger boat rescued them. They had no water, no food, and no restrooms, just fear, a hot sun all day, and a cold moon all night. It was the description of the cold moon that really got to Ruth; she didn't feel sorry for the girl, or pity her. She just felt as though she knew something *real* about her. Ruth could picture a tiny, dark-haired little girl staring at a big moon on the ocean. And she knew without a doubt that she wanted to admit a person who would share something so big, and so real, with a total stranger.

But this doesn't mean you need to mine the depths of your worst experiences, or manufacture one. You just need to share something that really mattered to you—and try to keep a modicum of perspective when you do so. Another applicant Ruth had, for example, wrote an entire essay on how the death of her pet turtle was the most impactful moment of her life. It wasn't a metaphor; it wasn't a complex allusion to contemporary politics; it was literally just an essay about the loss of her reptile. And it wasn't funny; she didn't sell it, or make it real. To Ruth, it seemed like the girl was simply saying, "Here is my essay about something sad that happened . . . that's what you want, right?" And it's not about the sad, although sad moments can be great material; it's about finding the moments or experiences you can really, truly describe.

The best way to become a more effective writer is to read, read, read, and read some more. You'll want to devour as many nonfiction essays as you can before you write your own statements; they'll inspire you, teach you, guide you, and entertain you. For great contemporary nonfiction essays, we recommend checking out the archives of *The New Yorker* magazine online, at newyorker .com. We also love *Granta*, a literary journal available from your local

library; Timothy McSweeney's Internet Tendency, at mcsweeneys
.net (where you can also find information about 826 Valencia's
free writing and tutoring centers, located in many major cities);
and we're also very partial to *Consider the Lobster*, a collection of
essays by the late David Foster Wallace.

Why I'm interested in University X

You might be asked to detail exactly why you'd like to attend
University X. A general statement that could be applied to all the
places you are applying to, such as, "I want a strong liberal arts
program with the opportunity for study abroad" is not nearly as
persuasive as one that directly addresses the attributes of the
school you are applying to. The following example is much more
convincing:

> I am very interested in the possibility of double majoring in
> math and music, and St. Olaf's strengths in those programs,
> as well as the curricular structure that allows for double
> majoring, are a perfect fit. Added to that is the opportunity
> to do a year-long study abroad combining the two and to
> participate in the sustainability initiatives on campus.

Get specific, and don't worry about BS-ing a little bit; you have
the right to change your mind once you get on campus, and no one
is going to hold you to the statements you make on your application.

Also reference any personal interactions you might have had
with the campus, admission counselors, alumni, or staff and faculty members. Again, this lets the campus know that you're truly
interested—not just sending off one of three dozen applications.

Supplementing the application: What they don't ask for, but would love to see

*Remember, admission officers are human beings, just like anyone
else.* Cover letters are great, if you an attach an additional document, or print it out and forward it to the admission office. If you've

got a portfolio to submit, do so electronically; make sure you're using the requested file formats. For video of any kind, post it on YouTube or Vimeo, send a link with a description of the video, and make sure it doesn't connect to anything ridiculous or inappropriate. What constitutes "ridiculous"? Well, for example, Carol's son and his friends built a potato gun in high school, and liked to take pictures of themselves shooting spuds into the river. Thankfully, this was in the days before Facebook and YouTube, but ridiculous things also include:

- Personal video diaries.
- Anything in which you swear or use profane language.
- Images or video of you doing anything illegal.
- If you have to ask, it's not appropriate.

Make sure your profiles on social networking websites are clean and appropriate, and that links don't have meta titles that include profane or inappropriate language.

If, for any reason, you need to send any paper documents, USB drives, or CDs in the mail, include a handwritten note, in blue or black ink, that states the following:

Please consider the attached project, my [charity work, art project, video essay, class project, etc.], as a supplement to my application. Thank you for taking the time to add it to my file.
Best,
Your name
Your address
Your high school
Your email or application #, if applicable.

If you do get the chance to meet with an admission officer, faculty member, or alum for an interview, always send a handwritten thank-you note, thanking that person for his or her time, and try to include a personalized comment about how much you enjoyed your conversation or interview. We're serious about this; students rarely send them anymore, and it will absolutely help you stand out. Remember: no glitter, no smiley faces, no stickers, and no swearing.

Addressing slip-ups in an extra essay

If you had one of those semesters in high school during which you messed up left and right, you may be thinking about trying to sweep it under the rug. *Don't*. Just like any corporate disaster or malfeasance, the worst thing you can do is stonewall and pretend it didn't happen. Your best option is to demonstrate your maturity, and address it head-on in a separate essay or letter. Sometimes there are good excuses, such as your health or that of a family member; sometimes, people just make bad decisions. *Everyone* makes mistakes, and admission officers have seen them all. Whatever it is, own up to it, and try to address what you've learned from it.

For family issues, lay them out. Be completely direct and honest, especially with the ones that are embarrassing and painful. Mom in prison? Dad in rehab? Did your younger sister pull a Bristol Palin and now there's a baby in the house? Think of this letter as an opportunity to demonstrate maturity; you're not looking for pity, just understanding. Believe us, everyone's got family problems, and your admission officer will likely empathize with you.

For your own personal bad choices, there's a whole range. Some of the most common slip-ups include the following:

- Did you choose a low-impact course selection (i.e., slacking off)? Does it look as if you're taking the senoritis train to Lazytown? If you are, own up to it. If not and, for example, you've exhausted all the tougher courses, then explain that.
- Did you choose extracurriculars over academics? Susie Senior loves her extracurriculars, and her grades suffered as a result. Or maybe Susie just recognized that her strengths don't always lie in a

classroom. Talk about the choices you've made, and try to advocate for yourself.

- Did you ignore your DARE class and smoke yourself right off the golf team? If you've made some really bad choices and wound up tossed off a team or extracurricular, then be up front about it. Explain what you did, or maybe even why you thought (or didn't think at all) it was a good idea at the time, and what you've learned as a result. You don't need to spout 12-step rhetoric to prove you're off the pot or spiced rum or whatever it was; just be honest, and emphasize that you understand that drugs or illegal substances interfered with your education, and that you won't let it happen ever again.

If colleges ask for *anything* else—like a seventh semester transcript, letter of recommendation from a math teacher (because of that D in your junior year, for example), or an additional writing sample, comply ASAP. If you can't return anything on time, your admission counselor will not be impressed.

Before you send off your applications, make sure that you have a qualified adult—like a teacher or your high school guidance counselor—look at your application and any additional materials you might be sending in.

Once you're done with your applications, take a month (or two) off. Just relax. You don't need to take any more steps (including visiting) until you've been accepted.

Making the Choice:
An Apples-to-Apples Comparison

CONGRATULATIONS! YOU'VE BEEN accepted to more than one place, and now you've got to choose. If you've got the time and the inclination, we do recommend visiting. An on-campus visit not only allows you to make the final gut decision about your preferences, but it often allows you to connect with the financial aid office, and possibly appeal for a higher aid award. However, before you take that step, you've got to look at your aid offers, and do the math to figure out what each school will actually cost you.

Don't just accept the first offer you receive; wait to hear from each school. You've got until May 1 to decide. No need to jump the gun; collect all your aid offers together and then use the following charts to understand what they mean.

In nearly every chapter, we've discussed the cost of attendance (COA). All colleges report their COAs to College Navigator (nces .ed.gov/collegenavigator), and most will list their COAs on their own websites as well. The COA is the absolute largest estimate that the college could make about how much each year will cost you. The COA includes Direct Costs (tuition, room and board, and fees) as well as books, spending money, travel costs, and other personal expenses. And although Direct Costs are generally outside of your control, you *do* have a fair amount of power over how you manage your other costs: books, spending money, travel and personal expenses. You can choose to have a $4 on-campus latte every day, or not; you can choose to buy new or used books; or you can choose to take a bus, plane, or carpool home for school holidays. A review we conducted of College Navigator shows that colleges estimate those other costs at anywhere from $700 to $4,100, and in order to *really* understand where your various aid offers stand, you've got to parse those "other" costs from the actual Direct Costs.

You'll also need to remember that the self-help you've been "awarded"—loans and work study—is *optional*. You don't have to take on the full amount of loans; you can choose to take on any amount.

The simplest way to understand what each school "really" costs is to make a chart that compares each school's direct costs and aid offers. You can find each school's Direct Costs at College Navigator, on the college's website, or sometimes on your aid award itself.

The following chart is an example. We've included blank charts on pages 209 and 210. Feel free to enter one college in "College E" to get the hang of it, and then fill out your own chart once you've got a handle on the math.

Direct Costs	College A	College B	College C	College D	College E
Tuition + Fees	40,004	31,760	24,300	17,616	
Room + Board	10,480	7,900	6,700	7,444	
Total Direct Costs	50,484	39,660	31,000	25,060	
Less Funded Aid (not including loans)	18,000	15,000	15,000	8,000	
= Net Direct Price	32,484	24,660	16,000	17,060	—

In this case, Susie Senior and her family can expect to pay $32,484 at College A, and $17,060 at College D, with a spread in between. But that's not the whole story; this chart doesn't break down the ways your family is planning to pay, and it doesn't include the student's contribution. We also haven't calculated what you'll spend on those "other" costs. Next, we'll calculate the total cost of attendance with both Direct Costs and Other Costs, and determine what you and your family can afford to pay out of pocket.

	College A	College B	College C	College D	College E
Net Direct Price	32,484	24,660	16,000	17,060	—
Books/supplies	1,100	1,080	1,400	980	
Personal spending	700	1,200	1,200	850	
Travel/transport	1000	500	500	500	
Total Costs	35,284	27,440	19,100	19,390	
Payments					
Parents					
From income	6,000	6,000	6,000	6,000	
From savings	5,000	5,000	5,000	5,000	
Student					
From savings/ summer	5,000	5,000	5,000	5,000	
Total payments	16,000	16,000	16,000	16,000	
Costs - payments = Gap	19,284	11,440	3,100	3,390	

We've given different costs for different colleges based on location, travel, and cost of living. When you complete this chart, do the following:

- Estimate books and supplies using the college's own data, posted on their website.
- Have a discussion about personal spending and what's acceptable for the nine-month school year.

You can also use the college's own estimates, although you certainly don't have to. For Colleges A and D, we're assuming Susie Senior's got a relative in the area who can cook her the occasional home-cooked meal and give her rides; for B and C, she's all on her own.

- Estimate your own travel costs using a flight aggregator site like Kayak.com, Amtrak.com for train prices, and Greyhound.com for bus prices (or any number of the coastal Chinatown-to-Chinatown bus services). Use the lowest price point possible.

The gap that you've calculated here is what you'll need to cover annually with loans and work-study. Remember: Before you take on *any* loans, you'll need to do the math for all four years, and calculate your repayment. (See Chapter 3 for more information.) After you've determined how much you'd be willing to take in loans, you'll need to look at your individual aid awards, and determine what you're eligible for at each college, using the following chart.

How to Meet the Gap	College A	College B	College C	College D	College E
Gap Amount	19,284	11,440	3,100	3,390	
Student Direct Loan	5,500	5,500	3,100	3,390	
Student Work Study	2,500	3,000	0	0	
Other sources	0	0	0	0	
Total	8,000	8,500	3,100	0	
Disparity	11,284	2,940	0	0	

Remember: You don't have to enter *all* the loans you're eligible for; you may also enter the amount of loans you're *willing* to take on. You should understand the *total* amount of the loan over four years, which includes interest, and what your monthly payments should be, if you haven't already. Go to Finaid.org and use the loan calculator to discover the total loan amount and calculate your monthly payments. If there's still a disparity, and the school in question is a college you'd really like to attend, consider either upping your loans, asking your parents to take out a Parent PLUS loan (see Chapter 5), or appealing (either now or when you visit). We discuss the appeal and the visit later in this chapter.

Here's a set of blank charts. If you run out of room, just re-create them on a sheet of scratch paper.

Step 1: Calculate Direct Costs Using College Navigator

Direct Costs	College A	College B	College C	College D	College E
Tuition + Fees					
Room + Board					
Total Direct Costs					
Less Funded Aid (not including loans)					
= Net Direct Price					

Step 2: Calculate Other Costs and Out-Of-Pocket Payment and Gap

	College A	College B	College C	College D	College E
Net Direct Price					
Books/supplies					
Personal spending					
Travel/transport					
Total Costs					

Payments					
Parents					
From income					
From savings					
Student					
From savings/ summer					
Total payments					
Costs - payments = Gap					

Step 3: Calculate Loans, Work Study, and the Final Disparity

How Meet the Gap	College A	College B	College C	College D	College E
Gap Amount					
Student Direct Loan					
Student Work Study					
Other sources					
Total					
Disparity					

Appealing your financial aid award

Not all colleges will accept or process an appeal, but it doesn't hurt to ask. When they *do* process an appeal, it's usually for one of two reasons: You've had a demonstrable change in your financial circumstances since the filing of the FAFSA, or you've got a better offer from another school that they may be willing to match or exceed. When we say "match," we mean that you're asking for your award to be adjusted to match the final net price. In order to appeal, you'll have to contact the financial aid office directly. There may be instructions about this on your aid award paperwork, but if not, you should email.

Your aid award should include the contact information for your financial aid officer, or the office itself. If it doesn't, contact the admission office, and let them know that you'd like to file an appeal of your aid award. If you have a reason—job loss since the filing of the FAFSA or any other family emergency—say so. It's also possible that you've received a better aid award from another school, and you'd like to know if the college in question can match it. The best way to do this is through email; use the following templates. We've got two here. One is for a documented family financial loss, and one is for award comparison. *Obviously, you should only appeal to your first-choice college.*

For a documented financial loss or other circumstance

Dear [Admission or Financial Aid Office/r, whatever contact you have available],

I was thrilled to receive my offer of admission and aid award from [College X], and I would very much like to accept. However, I would like to file an appeal of my financial aid award. As of [insert date], our family financial circumstances have changed due to [job loss, medical emergency, or other financial issue]. I am willing and able to document this, and I am very committed to enrolling in [College X], but cannot do so without a financial aid award adjustment. Would it be possible to file an appeal, or ask for a review of my award? Again, I am fully committed to enrolling, and I would be heartbroken if I was not able to accept your offer of admission.

Thank you for your time and assistance.

Best,

[Your name and contact information]

For aid offer matching

> Dear [Admission or Financial Aid Office/r, whatever contact you have available],
>
> I was thrilled to receive my offer of admission and aid award from [College X], and I would very much like to accept. However, I have received another, larger offer from [College Y], and although [College X] is still my first choice, my family cannot afford to enroll me. Would you consider increasing my aid so that my net price is the same as [College Y]? Again, I am fully committed to enrolling and [College X] is my number one choice, and I would be heartbroken if I was not able to accept your offer of admission and enroll. I've included a photocopy of [College Y]'s offer. Please let me know what you require on our end for additional documentation.
>
> Thank you for your time and assistance.
>
> Best,
>
> [Your name and contact information]

Note: Do not forget to include a photocopy of the offer from College Y.

Appealing *after* you visit

If possible, you may want to consider appealing after you've visited. Visiting will serve two purposes:

1. Allow you to discover where you really, really want to go.
2. Allow you to connect in person with admission, the financial aid office, and faculty members.

Don't underestimate the power of a personal connection! Although you can't force it, if you can get an admission officer or financial aid officer on your side, you may be more successful in your appeal.

Read on for more information about the visit, and how you may be able to make a personal contact.

The campus visit

The visit can be the number-one deciding factor for most families and can often influence decisions about cost and loan burdens. Because of this, we recommend that you *first* calculate where you're getting the best offer, and *then* set up a visit; it'll prevent you from falling in love with a college you cannot afford.

College campuses are electric. There's something to be said for the simple effect of putting a bunch of quick-thinking minds in the same geographic space; it's exciting in a way that the working world is not. There's a real energy to a campus, and that energy is different at each one. Although it is possible (and certainly easiest) to visit on a weekend, we don't recommend it, because students won't actively be going to class. You want to see the campus as it is during the week. The best possible time to visit is on a weekday, when school is in session.

We recommend that you take at least one parent with you, and plan as far in advance as you can. One of your parents may need to take a personal day from work. You'll want to prepare a list of questions for the college, or just use one of our favorite resources, "A Pocket Guide to Choosing a College," from the National Survey of Student Engagement. It's available for free, in English or in Spanish, from nsse.indiana.edu and all of the questions are great ones. Bring a notebook with you so you can write down the answers, and collect contact information from the people you meet with.

You'll also want to consider the costs of the visit. Can you drive? Do you need to take a bus or a train? Will you need to stay overnight in a hotel? Often, colleges offer an overnight for prospective students, at which you can bunk up with a current freshman or sophomore. We *highly* recommend an overnight—they're so fun, and they allow you to *really* connect with the student body. But if your parent is accompanying you or there's no overnight on offer, he or she is not going to want to sleep in a dorm room. Most colleges will make prospy (prospective student) deals with local hotels or motels; check the website, or call the admission office, to find out what those offers might be. If not, we recommend using kayak.com, a flight and hotel aggregator, or simply calling the hotel in question and inquiring about a prospective student rate. Many hotels—particularly those in large college towns—will have package deals for prospective students and their families. If your child's going to be there for four years, they want your business!

For each campus visit, be prepared to spend on:

- Gas, train, or airfare to get you to and from.
- A taxi to and from the airport, if necessary.
- Meals. Most colleges will spot you at least one meal in the dining halls, but for the others, you've got to be prepared.

Don't spend your money on:

- Merchandise! Oh, those bookstores with their over-priced Hanes sweatshirts are so enticing. But you might not have made your final decision yet—or received your final offer. Are you really ready to commit to that $55 sweatshirt?

You've generally got two options for a campus visit: a group visit, or a private visit.

The group visit

All schools host "group visit" or "campus visit" days that are open to everyone, and include just about everything you can think of. They're usually held on weekday holidays, such as Veteran's Day or Martin Luther King Day, which is a wonderful advantage for travel. The drawback? School isn't in session, and although the group visit is almost overwhelmingly informative, there's little to no personal attention.

Here's a sample of what a group visit might entail:

- 9:00: Welcome speech! Often, the President of the college will greet you.

- 9:15: Faculty speech. Colleges love to show off their top dogs. This is usually pretty entertaining.
- 9:30: The Dean of Admission will probably give you a marketing speech that will differentiate the college from the competition. He or she will tell you what "makes them different," without giving specific comparisons to other schools.
- 9:45: The Director of Admission will give you the nitty gritty about the application process.
- 10:00: Students and parents will split up. Students head to a student-only discussion, which is always fun and very candid. It's often the best part of the talking heads lineup, and your parents are out of the room. Now is the time to ask about where the best parties are.
- Parents will head to a separate panel and ask the tough questions about safety, security, and on-campus healthcare. Colleges are required by a federal law, the Cleary Act, to provide actual crime statistics. You should be able to get a brochure about crime statistics in print or online. Obviously, they don't put this brochure in your visit packet—you've got to ask for it.
- 11:00: Campus Tour, led by trained current students.
- 12:00: Lunch, probably in one of the dining halls. If it's catered, that's a sign that their food may be terrible, so ask your student host about the dining halls.
- 1:00: Concurrent Programs. Divide and conquer with your parent(s). These should include:
  - Financial aid.
  - Career services.
  - International education/Study abroad.
  - Housing.
  - Special programs (Honors Program, etc.).
- 2:30: Individual appointments in Admission and Financial Aid. If they *don't* offer this, *ask for it in*

advance of your visit. Some schools won't take individual appointments on group visit days. If that's the
case, skip the group visit, and go for a private visit, on
another day. On a professional note, we consider this
lousy customer service, and it may be a symptom of a
pervasive attitude at the institution.

That's a typical schedule for a group visit, and it's a great plan
for a school that may not be your first choice. Your parents usually
won't have to take off work to attend, and you won't have to take
off school. However, we really recommend, for your top two or
even three choices, that you set up a private visit. All colleges offer
private visits, and they're the ideal way to see the campus. They're
all about *you*, not just a song-and-dance lineup for the masses. The
only drawback is that you, and your parents, will have to take off
a weekday.

The private visit

The itinerary of a private visit may look like this:

- 9:00: You'll arrive at the admission office, and have
  a general session or interview with the admission
  counselor assigned to you. You're interviewing them,
  and they're interviewing you. Ask good questions;
  as we mentioned earlier, we *love* the "Pocket Guide
  to Choosing a College," from the National Survey of
  Student Engagement. It's available for free, in English
  or in Spanish, from nsse.iub.edu. If you ask good questions, you'll impress them. Take notes, and be atten-
  tive, respectful, and polite—it isn't more complex
  than that, despite what other books might tell you. We
  recommend that you meet *alone* with the admission
  counselor, and ask your parents to wait outside—it'll
  give you a chance to shine, and also give your parents
  an opportunity to ask their *own* questions.

- 10:00: Individual campus tour with a student.

- 11:00: You'll likely sit in on a class. Choose something you're interested in!

- 12:00: Lunch with a current student.

- 1:00: You'll meet with a financial aid officer.

- 2:00: You'll meet with other campus specialists, such as coaches, music faculty, and so on.

- 3:00: You'll have an exit interview with your admission counselor. If you need to appeal your award, we actually recommend that you *don't* bring this up now. Wait a few days, send a handwritten thank-you note, and then follow up with a written request for an aid appeal a week or two later. They'll remember you, and they won't feel blindsided.

If the admission dean or director comes out to greet you—just to say "Hello," or "Welcome"—that's a great sign. It means they're really interested in *you*.

Hopefully, you'll be able to narrow down your options by figuring out the final net price, your loans and work study, and making a visit to campus. We've helped you figure out the cost; the rest of the decision is up to you and your family. However, sometimes, things don't work out the way you want them to. If you're not able to appeal a truly unhelpful aid award, or you simply can't afford any of your options, don't panic. It's not going to be the end of the world if you don't go to college right away, and if you take an extra year, either at a community college or working and volunteering, you might be able to bring down the price at your college of choice if you re-apply as a stronger applicant. Read the next chapter to find out more.

An Intentional Alternative Plan

IF YOU CRUNCHED the numbers in Chapter 10 and discovered that you'll have to take on an excess of $8,000 per year in student loans in order to go to college, it's time to think again. If you can't meet our $8K Debt Challenge, you likely cannot afford to go to college this fall. Sure, the *loans* are there; there are eager lenders on every single college website, popping up through insidious little boxes like the "SimpleTuition" ads on the Princeton Review, showing up in your inbox, and yes, still through the mail. But unless you're planning on majoring in math or one of the hard sciences (and there's *absolutely no way* you'll change your mind or major), you're at a statistical disadvantage—your risk will likely garner no reward. By taking on more debt than you'll be able to repay, all you're doing is handicapping yourself. We *promise* you that's the truth. We can't stress it enough. If you haven't read Chapter 3, go back and take a look.

If you're from a family background that isn't financially stable, you might think that taking on college debt will be your ticket to security. But if you exceed $8K in student debt per year, you could end up in worse shape than you've ever been. Instead of an express elevator to the top floor, your debt will be a cartoon anvil attached to your ankle. It'll pull you out the window and down 25 stories into the street. College, for now, may have to remain a dream instead of a reality.

But before you collapse at the kitchen table with an uncontrollable sob, hear us out: We've got an (intentional) alternative plan for you to consider.

There are dozens of reasons that you could be unable to meet our $8K Debt Challenge, but we're guessing they fall into one of two categories:

1.   Your academic credentials didn't make the cut. You got senioritis—or junioritis, or sophomoritis, or freshman-itis. Whatever it was, at some point, you stopped caring about your grades, or you weren't able to do very well on the SAT or ACT. We understand; high school is *boring*. Sitting in an uncomfortable chair for eight hours a day reading dull textbooks is no way to learn (although it's not as though *we* have a better solution for public education), and some students are just better at sucking it up and running the gauntlet than others. That's really what getting through high school is about: endurance. Not ability; not IQ; not natural talent—straight-up endurance. And if you got lazy or slacked off, your grades probably suffered, and so did your test scores.

2.   You've applied to colleges at which your credentials only qualified you for admission—but not for any merit aid. In other words, you weren't even close to being the best, or one of the best, in the class.

Your life starts *now*. You're about to have a fresh start. Get ready to embrace it—even if it's not at your dream school just yet.

We're so sorry to tell you that you can't go to college this fall; we can almost see your face through the pages, and your parents' faces as they read this chapter, perhaps reflecting on their own debt, and wondering how they can break the news to you. But this is *not the worst thing in the world*. It will actually be wonderful for you—just wait, and you'll see. Our intentional alternative plan is actually kind of fun.

Tomorrow morning (or whenever the next business day is), you're going to wake up and call the admission officer at your top three choices—the ones you can't afford. And you're going to tell that admission officer that you simply can't afford to start as a freshman, but you're going to go to your local community college for the next year or two, starting *this summer*. Yes, we mean this summer, as in the one after you graduate from high school. Look on the bright side: At least you won't have to work as much—and some of your classmates will be doing the same exact thing. Ask that admission officer to send you a list of what community colleges they take credit from, and for what courses. Ask if they give scholarships to transfer students, and find out what GPA you'll need to qualify for one. You'll need to make a plan and you will need to think about each class you enroll in. And you're going to live at home, without a car. Get rides. Take the bus. Get a bicycle (they're really good for you)! If you have a car, you're going to sell it. "Well," you might be thinking, "how am I going to get to work?"

You'll take the bus to work, just like millions of people without cars do. But you're not going to work very much; at most, you should work 10 to 15 hours a week at a part-time job. Why? Because you're going to be devoting most of your energy to getting As in every single course that you take at a community college, and you're going to ask your parents to help you. In Chapter 7 we estimated that nine hours a week at $10 per hour for 52 weeks should generate enough income after taxes to pay the average cost of community college: $3,440.

If you've slacked off in high school, they likely slacked off with you. Now is the time to change. Your parents are going to start quizzing you weekly, helping you with flashcards and essays, and giving you rides to and from class. For this year, your number-one priority is getting As in *every single community college course you take*. But don't worry; community college is not that hard. You can absolutely do it. If 90-year-old women who didn't learn to read until they left the family farm at age 20 can do it, so can you. That's the beauty of community colleges: They are structured to teach everyone, regardless of age, ability, or background. They are, first and foremost, places to *learn*. Your instructors and professors are there because they really want to help you learn—and you will absolutely learn something. You might find, especially if you've been slacking off, that it feels really good to learn something and get good grades.

It's important to start as soon as you can at a community college, preferably during the first summer session. That way, you're maximizing the number of grades you can report when you re-apply as a transfer student to your dream colleges. If you know that you still won't cut it at those schools, use our MAP to find colleges that *will* fund you. It's time to change your dreams—but that doesn't mean shattering them. There are so many wonderful ways to *be* in the world, and setting your sights on different goals doesn't mean giving up—it means being smart. Remember: When you graduate from college, you'll get to do something *amazing*. Those amazing things could include:

- Getting the classic Eurail pass and bumming around Paris, Prague, or Rome for a few months.
- Teaching English in Japan or Korea (and no, they don't pay you very much).
- Working for the Peace Corps and aiding impoverished communities throughout the globe (they *really* don't pay you very much).
- Starting your own arts project out of an Airstream trailer and traveling the country. (Will you be paying yourself? Maybe not . . . but you'll need gas money.)
- Touring with your band.
- Following someone you love halfway across the world.
- Taking an unpaid internship working for a person or publication you've worshipped (you'll have to work part-time for pay).

- Living on a houseboat in Amsterdam working for
  Greenpeace (making just enough to eat, but hey, you'll
  be living your ideals).

Those are real things that real students we've known did right after they graduated from college. And if they had to worry about paying off a huge student loan payment, they wouldn't have been able to do any of those things. They'd be living at home with their parents, working in coffee shops or restaurants, or as nannies, like other, less fortunate students we've known. Or they're working jobs they hate just to pay the bills.

Living at home with your parents for the next year won't be so bad. We promise. *Under no circumstances whatsoever should you move out and get your own apartment*; it's a waste of money. If your parents were counting on your absence, try to make a deal: What can you offer? Childcare for a younger sibling or assistance for an older relative? Home repair? Double the chores? Negotiate, negotiate, negotiate. Now is *not* the time to start paying rent.

If you can't meet our $8K Debt Challenge, we recommend that you try our intentional alternative plan. The end of the game is your college degree. No one ever asks what college you started *at*; they just ask where you graduated *from*. The point isn't how you get to your diploma—it's getting there that really counts.

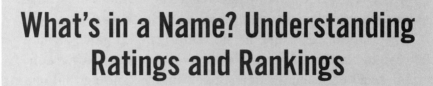

What's in a Name? Understanding Ratings and Rankings

COLLEGE RATINGS AND rankings assess the "good," the "better," and the "best." They are an inevitable byproduct of higher education; if we're paying for college with our money, our time, and our energy, we'd like to know what the "best" colleges are. And why shouldn't we? Our time and energy aside, college tuition has grown at a faster rate than *healthcare* costs. Measuring the lifetime value of that expense is an incredibly worthwhile enterprise for the consumer, and we encourage you to investigate the available data about your intended major or career path and ideal colleges as thoroughly as you can before you sign on the dotted line. Throughout this book, we've repeatedly quoted a study from PayScale.com, a website that tracks compensation data, to indicate that bachelor's degrees from some colleges and universities *do* have an enormous dollar value—and many do not. But PayScale's study isn't *anything* like the rankings books, which is why we like it so much. It's a simple calculation of the dollar value of a bachelor's degree. Rankings and ratings lists *do not* calculate that, no matter what they imply.

For many people, particularly anyone who wants to major in the humanities or soft sciences, college isn't—and *cannot* be—just about the dollar value of the degree. We asked Carol's daughter, who majored in English at a large public university, what her college experience meant to her:

> The best parts of my college years were the ones when I was writing and I really felt that I knew what I was talking about; when the culmination of lectures (seemingly irrelevant at the time), notes, readings, and gallery visits resulted in the ability to create at least one apt paragraph. I arrived occasionally at a state of understanding that one of my professors described as "a place most of us get to for 15 seconds a year, if we're lucky." And I was lucky.
>
> At some point, I felt that everything I saw in the world was a part of everything I was learning. Connections and cross-references bubbled up in every conversation and just walking down the street. The world became an infinite echo chamber of productive thoughts and phrases. I saw my intellectual heroes lurking behind phrases and arguments in everything—politics, fiction and nonfiction, advertising, et cetera. The leaders of my life of the mind came to life themselves once I realized that their theories, arguments, thoughts, and expressions had built the world around me.

Ruth's daughter majored in engineering at a mid-size private university in the Midwest. Her take on her experience is as follows.

> My biggest takeaway from studying a hard science at the undergraduate level was one that took me a while to realize, but ultimately empowered me once I did. College did not just teach me how to solve calculus problems, or how to diagnose what was wrong with my oscilloscope in lab. Rather, engineering school taught me how to take seemingly huge and unapproachable problems and break them down into chewable, solvable pieces. Every problem you

come across in engineering school is one you haven't seen before, and that can be daunting. But once you learn how to break that problem down into smaller problems you know you can attempt, you truly become able—as a scientist, and as an adult attempting to make their way through life after college. Just as problems in engineering school are difficult and huge, such are problems in life, and I am grateful my education prepared me so well to tackle life problems.

I also feel I owe some of my success to the college community in which I was privileged to be a part of. Having gone to a mid-size private school, I had different experiences than some of my peers at larger universities. For example, when I was walking between classes I liked the familiarity we all shared—that you could walk to class and usually see someone you knew, but you wouldn't always see someone you felt obligated to say hi to. That was a nice balance. I was also fortunate to have the opportunity to become close with some of my professors and mentors in a way that may or may not have been possible at a larger university.

You might have noticed that neither woman talked about where her degree has "gotten her" in the world, but rather what it gave her, personally and intellectually, while she was in school. There's no way to quantify that kind of engagement. It's a qualitative issue, rather than a quantitative one.

Nonetheless, we want to know what our investment is going to get us—and the industry of higher education is ready to sell us an answer, even one that's only half-true. The whole truth is that it's impossible to assess the real and total value of colleges in any given study. Trust us; we've tried. There is so much more to a college education than the *numbers* we can crunch; there is engagement (short and long term; micro and macro), there is professional success and satisfaction (without a lot of money), there is friendship, there is love, there is participation, and above all, there is intellectual satisfaction. And the biggest uncertainty of all is *who you are*; identity is nebulous. Where do *you* stop and your *education* begins? We just don't know the real answer to that. Statistically, we can say that the rich are different; students from wealthy families are better "achievers" than other kinds of students. But who is defining achievement? Is it really just about grades? And where does that leave everyone who *doesn't* come from a wealthy family? What comes out of the classroom, across the board and for every kind of student, is something that every single facet of education tries to calculate, and it can't. If it could, we'd have perfect public schools with 100 percent graduation rates. But we don't. We simply cannot do the math on an *experience*. That means that ratings and rankings are in many ways a near-perfect conflict of logic; they assess an experience that is definitively qualitative and relativistic (that is, the development of critical thinking) in a quantitative and hierarchical manner.

Or, to put it differently: Ask any college professor, "Who is better? Kant or Jung? Plato or Socrates? Barthes or Foucault? Henry Field or Alan Turing?"

There's no right answer, they'll tell you; the very premise of your question, that one kind of knowledge or thinking can be "better" than another, is impossible in a post-structuralist intellectual environment like the one we have now. Asking "Who is better?" is literally the opposite of the purpose of higher education, which is to see the world in shades of complexity and nuance, in shades of *gray*, rather than in black and white. There is no "better" shade of gray; there are only *different* shades of gray.

If college were free, and required very little time or emotional investment on the part of the student, then professors everywhere could decry the *U.S. News & World Report* and the *Princeton Review* and so on as truly meaningless analyses of the relativistic experience. They could simply throw those rankings in the trash and be done with it. But college is not free; as we've said, over and over throughout this book, it's extraordinarily expensive. And rankings, too, are big business; those books and websites aren't free. You've got to pay for them, either for a hardbound copy of the books themselves or for full access to the websites and their data.

You want an answer, so like anything else, someone is willing to sell you one. But that doesn't mean it's the entire answer.

Ruth was on the *U.S. News & World Report* College Rankings board for 13 years, beginning when she was director of admission at Ball State University, and through her time as director of admission at the University of Illinois Urbana/Champaign. The rankings advisory board is made up of admission directors and deans from all over the country, who pay their own expenses to attend meetings to review the methodology for the rankings and provide feedback. Seventy-five percent of the rankings are calculated using data collected annually by the federal government, known as IPEDs; that data is available online for free, either at nces.ed.gov or nces.ed.gov/collegenavigator. That data includes two primary components:

1. **Input data**: This means the makeup of the most recent incoming freshman class—GPA, test scores, etcetera. This might tell us how difficult it may be to gain admission, but it doesn't tell us anything about the quality of the education after four years (or even one semester).

2. **Asset, or resource, data**: This includes the size of the endowment, the number of faculty, the number of books in the library, the value of the physical property, and so on. Does a $10 million parcel of land on a river really make the education better? Probably not. But, it's got a dollar value, so it's part of the formula.

The remaining 22.5 percent is simply personal opinions; college presidents and admission directors were asked what they *thought* about other schools in an annual survey. It's that simple—and, in a way, that irresponsible. No one can know *all* the schools in the running, of course. What they do know, quite simply, are the most well-known schools. It's a popularity contest, plain and simple.

What we'd like you to understand about input data, in particular, is that it says absolutely nothing about the school itself—it only says something about the academic backgrounds of the students. It's a correlation—*not* a causality. It's not a guarantee of anything, other than that the schools that top the list are thought highly of by other academics. If you're not an academic, does it really matter? There's no way to know—and it's certainly not worth banking on with student loans. If it comes down to a brand-versus-price scenario—and your understanding of brand is informed by a rankings list—please check PayScale.com's ROI study for an assessment of that college's return on investment.

On the other end of the spectrum, the *Princeton Review* and *Forbes* create their own annual rankings, using different types of data that focus primarily on current, not just incoming, students. The *Princeton Review* rankings come from an 80-question survey of more than 122,000 current students conducted online; current students are defined as those who have a valid university email address. The questions in the survey range from campus life and academics, to the student's thoughts on fellow student's attitudes and opinions. The catch? The *Princeton Review* only surveys students at 373 colleges, a list that is chosen by the board. At the end of the day, it's just a list they put together; it's not a calculation of every college (more than 4,400) in the country—not even close.

The *Forbes* rankings attempt to use quite a bit of alumni data, using salary, student loan burdens, default rates, graduation rates, competitive awards, and listings from "Who's Who in America" and the annual Forbes/CCAP Corporate Officers List. Its student satisfaction surveys come from RateMyProfessor.com, an academic Yelp, so to speak, and we think it is statistical garbage. And although the people in "Who's Who in America" and the Forbes/ CCAP Corporate Officers List are probably important and financially successful, they're not *everyone* who is important or successful. It's a limited group, one that, perhaps rightfully, reflects the *Forbes* worldview of corporate success and entitlement. So although we applaud them for using student loan burdens and graduation rates, we think you should take their ratings with a large handful of salt.

What ratings or rankings do we recommend that you use? Ideally, none of them. But we know you're going to, so please keep their methodologies in mind, and remember that rankings are *never* the whole truth. And although we've referred to PayScale's ROI survey quite frequently, to be fair, it's got problems too. From the tuition calculated (they use sticker price, not net price) to the inability to weight income by region of the country ($87 annually goes a lot farther in Montana than in Manhattan), not to mention the conclusion that the only kind of success is financial success, the PayScale ROI's got problems. But it *does* calculate something: the dollar value of a degree. If you're looking at an expensive brand, you should at least think about what it can give you in dollars— because there's no way to predict what it will give you in *sense*. We can't tell you who is going to give you the best education. It's like falling in love, and only you can figure that out. You'll know it when you see it—you'll feel energized and engaged, and you will *want* to participate.

13

What Color Is Your Passport? Advice for International Students

IN CHAPTER 2, we explained need, the Free Application for Federal Student Aid (FAFSA), the PROFILE, and other admittedly arcane federal processes, terminology, and acronyms—all of which are important for U.S. citizens, U.S. nationals, and eligible non-citizens. Eligible non-citizens generally include the following:

- U.S. permanent resident, with a Permanent Resident Card (I-551, formerly known as an Alien Registration Receipt Card or "Green Card").
- Conditional permanent resident (I-551C).
- Other eligible noncitizen with an Arrival-Departure Record (I-94) from the Department of Homeland Security showing any one of the following designations: "Refugee," "Asylum Granted," "Parolee" (I-94 confirms that you were paroled for a minimum of one year and status has not expired), T-Visa holder (T-1, T-2, T-3, etc.), or "Cuban-Haitian Entrant."

- The holder of a valid certification or eligibility letter from the Department of Health and Human Services showing a designation of "Victim of human trafficking."
- A resident of the Republic of Palau (PW), the Republic of the Marshall Islands (MH), or the Federated States of Micronesia (FM).
- A Canadian-born Native American under terms of the Jay Treaty.

All of these categories of student should have an Alien Registration Number, or ARN, to use the FAFSA. For more information about becoming an eligible non-citizen, or to obtain an ARN, you must contact the Social Security Administration, at ssa.gov.

If you're not any of those things, you're officially an international, or foreign, student: a citizen of a country other than the United States, and you won't be eligible for the aid we outlined in Chapter 2 (federal financial aid). You may have another different status, that of an undocumented student. If so, skip to Chapter 14 for information.

As an international student, you may still have to complete the PROFILE, and as you read on, we will detail extra forms and documents you will need to submit. For you and your family, parts of the college application process will be exactly the same (the merit or academic scholarship part), and other parts (the required forms) will be very different than that of the typical American student.

When a U.S. college or university offers admission to you, they will also send to you the documentation (an I-20 form) you need to obtain a visa to enter the United States for study. By sending an I-20 to you, that school is certifying that you have submitted to them documentation that demonstrates that you have the ability to benefit from your education, that you possess the funding to pay for your education, that you have a residence in another country to which you will return, and that you intend to depart from the United States at the conclusion of your program of study. Whew.

Buried in all of this is a very important word: *documentation*. Just as you will have to submit documents that prove your academic ability, such as certified copies of your high school transcript or the final results of your national school leaving exam and TOEFL or IELTS exam, you, and your parents, will have to submit *financial* documentation. If a college to which you applied asks for additional financial documents—submit them!

As we say throughout this book, the most important thing to remember about college in the United States is that it is very, very expensive. The U.S. Department of State estimates that there are only 1,000 international students each year who receive a "full ride" (a.k.a. a complete scholarship) as an undergraduate to a U.S. college. As of 2014–2015, there are more than 975,000 undergraduate international students in the United States. In searching websites, we found only 79 U.S. schools that consider offering full rides to international students. So be realistic about your chances. It's doubtful that you will be able to go to college in the U.S. for free.

What parts of the cost-based college search process are the same?

The answer is reassuring: most of them. Let's begin with that oh-so-important conversation you've got to have with your parents about money (if you haven't already, take a look at Chapter 4). As an international student, this is *doubly* important, because they'll likely be paying for your costs out of pocket, and you'll also need to document your financial circumstances for each college you apply to. You and your parents will have to submit truthful and accurate information about your financial situation and the resources you have to pay for college. If you're a parent who is reading this chapter for your child, please look at Chapter 5 as well.

The entire process you'll use to figure out what schools might be a good match for you remains the same, regardless of your citizenship status. Chapters 6 and 7 taught you how to look for merit scholarships at schools, and how to use the MAP to match your own strengths to schools. The processes colleges use to award merit aid remain the same, regardless of the nationality of the applicant.

Most of the materials you'll need to submit as a part of your application for admission and financial aid will be the same as those required of U.S. citizens. Good writing—the kind you will demonstrate in your essay—is not bound by any national borders. You'll be expected to display the same caliber of fluency and ability to use the English language as any native speaker. Nearly all classes in the United States *are* taught in English, excepting advanced coursework in foreign languages. Incidentally, if you cannot write well enough in English to submit an application essay, you will likely not succeed as a student.

Strong letters of reference, with certified translations attached if necessary, can speak volumes about personal qualities and abilities regardless of the nationality of the writer.

And making the effort to build a personal relationship with staff responsible at each school for admitting and giving scholarship dollars to foreign students is also something you must do. This is not optional.

Additionally, just like your fellow students who happen to be U.S. citizens, you should be making a dollar-to-dollar cost comparison before making your final choice of school, which we discussed in Chapter 11.

Chapter 12 is possibly even more important for those of you who do not live in the United States. There are more than 4,400 colleges and universities in the United States, and the odds are pretty good that you have never heard of most of them. You'll be tempted to turn to "external" evaluations to determine which are the "best," and we want to help you make that a useful experience.

What in the admission and financial aid process will be different for you?

Application for admission

It may be that the school in which you are interested has a different application form for use by international students. Part of the difference in this form is that it will be more user-friendly for recording non-U.S. addresses and contact information. If so, this will be *very* evident on the school's website, with a special tab/ section labeled for international students. If a school has a form for international students, by all means use it, or expect after completing and submitting the form for U.S. students to be asked to also complete the international student form.

Supplementary materials

If you are not from an English-speaking country, you will need to supply proof of your fluency in English, generally results of either the TOEFL or the IELTS test. Most schools will publish the minimum score required for each of these exams on their website. Go to the appropriate testing website to find information about testing dates and sites in your country: ets.org for the TOEFL and ielts .org for the IELTS. A few schools will also require you to take the SAT (bigfuture.collegeboard.org) or the ACT (act.org). If your home country has a national school-leaving exam, or if you've completed an IB or EB curriculum, you will need to have your predicted scores (for exams you will sit for at the end of the year) included as a part of the school report.

Secondary school transcripts and school report

You will need to submit official copies of your secondary school transcripts (records of courses taken and grades or scores earned), and perhaps certified translations as well. The school report is to be written by the principal, headmaster or headmistress, or career adviser at your school. And as much information as your school can provide about itself—enrollment, grading system, curriculum, placement of graduates, success with national school leaving exams—can all help to strengthen your application, so attach those to your application if they're available.

Financial aid

Good news: No FAFSA will be required of you. But you *will* need to submit either a completed institutional financial aid application (from the college itself) or a College Board PROFILE and the International Student Certification of Finances (bigfuture.college board.org). The PROFILE is explained in Chapter 2. The Certification of Finances will require a listing of *exact* amounts of assured and projected funding from your own money, your parents, sponsors, and the government of your home country. In addition to listing the amounts of money, you will need to have that amount certified by signature by an officer at your bank, signatures of those providing the money (your parents or sponsor), and a copy of the award letter for any funds from your home government. If you are offered admission, a copy of this form will be attached to your certificate of eligibility (I-20), which is the form you will take to a U.S. consulate or embassy to apply for a visa.

Here's where things become *really* different for you. A U.S. college or university *cannot* and *will not* admit you (and give you a Certificate of Eligibility I-20 form to apply for a visa) unless it has proof that you can not only succeed academically but also can afford to pay for your education. You *cannot* simply be admitted and then figure out how you are going to pay. You have to have either your own money, money from a sponsor, money from the college, or money from your home government or another agency to pay for your education. And you will have to prove that. There is no U.S. government or state funding for international students. Rather, the sources of financial support for you are:

- You and your family.
- The college or university.
- Private scholarship programs.
- Your home government for either grants or loans.

There are a limited number of colleges and universities that offer significant amounts of scholarship aid to international students. Remember: Even if they say they will fully fund international students, that's only if they choose to admit you. And "fully fund" does not mean that they will simply give you the money. You must demonstrate "need" as well; even though you are not completing the FAFSA you will be submitting other financial information. Whether or not general merit aid programs are available to international students is at the discretion of each individual college.

Student loans from either the U.S. government or most private lenders are not an option for international students. There are a few private lenders that offer student loans to international students. To our knowledge, most will require a cosigner who is either a U.S. citizen or a permanent resident. A cosigner agrees to take the same responsibility for paying the loan off that you do, and if you do not pay, they have to. This is a huge commitment and not one that someone will enter into lightly. Most of these are relatively expensive loan programs for which the interest rates float (adjust) to a rate that is tied to the LIBOR (London Inter Bank Offered Rate).

Your home country may have student grant or loan programs that you can apply for and use in the U.S. *Canadian students* may obtain loan funding through Service Canada (esdc.gc.ca).

Student employment (a job on campus) is a possibility, but the earnings will be minimal—perhaps only $2,000 to $3,000 per year. You cannot assume that a job will provide anything more than limited spending money. A small number of U.S. colleges and universities offer what is called "co-op" learning programs, during which students have the opportunity to work off-campus at a corporation for regular wages. Co-op placements are not available to international students until they have completed two terms of on-campus academic work. Jobs are not guaranteed and most require strong fluency in English.

The best source for information about college and university study in the United States in countries around the world is EducationUSA (educationusa.state.gov). This service of the U.S. Department of State is in every country in which the United States has a diplomatic presence, with both bricks and mortar embassies and offices, and virtual presences. Services from EducationUSA are free and include everything from internet access, to meeting with an educational advisor, to information about U.S. High Education Fairs in your home country. Take a look at the website to learn more.

Once you receive an offer of admission and an I-20, there is still no guarantee of being granted a visa to actually study in the United States. The U.S. consular or embassy officer will interview you, and may ask for additional documentation before issuing a visa. The current fee for a foreign student visa is $160 (U.S.). That is the fee for applying for a visa—there may be an issuance fee as well (assuming the visa is granted). The U.S. Department of State (travel.state.gov) has country-by-country information about process, processing times, interview schedules, and fees.

Our single best piece of advice for you is this: Find *your* admission counselors at each school in which you are interested, get in touch, and *stay* in touch. If there is funding for you to study at that school, they'll help you find it.

14

Are you a DREAMer? Advice for Undocumented Students

IF YOU ARE one of the 65,000 students who graduate from a U.S. high school each year but do not have either U.S. citizenship or permanent residency, you are considered to be undocumented. DREAMers, or individuals who meet the general requirements of the Development, Relief, and Education for Alien Minors Act, live in every state and hail from all over the globe. Though the DREAM Act has not yet passed as of this writing, the phrase has become synonymous with undocumented students who wish to remain in the United States.

You may have kept your immigration status a secret from many people in your life, including friends, teachers, coaches, and counselors at school, but when it comes to college you do not need to keep your status a secret from anywhere you choose to apply.

There is no federal law that prohibits the admission of undocumented immigrants to U.S. colleges and universities, public or private, nor does federal law require students to prove citizenship in order to enter U.S. institutions of higher education.

Again: There is no federal law that prohibits you from enrolling in any college or university.

Undocumented students are eligible for in-state tuition rates
at public colleges and universities in 18 of the 50 states, just like
any other bona fide resident of California or Texas or New York or
Utah or 14 others. In five of those 18 states (California, Minnesota,
New Mexico, Texas, and Washington), undocumented students are
eligible to receive state-funded financial aid. Only one state, South
Carolina, prohibits undocumented students from enrolling at state
colleges and universities, and three states, Arizona, Georgia, and
Indiana, specifically bar undocumented students from receiving
in-state tuition, but that still leaves more than 4,000 colleges and
universities that are possible, that want you as a student, and have
funding that is available to you.

The largest barrier for undocumented students is not legal,
but financial. As an undocumented student (whether you become
DACAmented and get a social security number or not; we'll get
to DACA in a bit), you *cannot become eligible for federal financial
aid programs like the Pell Grant and Direct Student Loans*, even
though your family's income will be assessed to find an expected
family contribution, or EFC (see Chapter 2 for more terminology),
using the FAFSA's calculations. You can use FAFSA4caster at any
time to estimate your EFC.

However, you are still eligible for scholarships that come from
the colleges themselves, and if you follow our MAP in Chapter 6
and apply only to colleges at which you are in the top 25 percent of
applicants, you should be able to afford to go. Our ongoing paradigm
of funded versus unfunded applies heavily in the circumstances of
undocumented students, because most merit aid programs (tuition
discounting or institutional scholarships; see Chapter 1 for further
explanation) are agnostic when it comes to immigration status.

Step 1: Start the search

To begin your search, you will need to follow the same process outlined in Chapters 6 and 7. First, create a list of possible

colleges using the listed criteria and then ask yourself: Do your academic credentials place you in the top 25 percent of enrolling students? Do the values of each college match your own passions and interests? Will it be financially feasible for you and your family to meet the EFC? (Helpful hint: If your Actual EFC, as calculated in Chapter 2, is much lower than your EFC, narrow your search to colleges at which you will be in the top 10 percent of incoming applicants.)

Once you have a list of schools, reach out to the admission office directly (as we suggest for all students) and ask about any policies or requirements they may have for undocumented students.

Step 2: Ask the admissions office four important questions

1. Will you be considered as a "domestic" student, or treated as an international student?
2. Are there additional forms or interviews?
3. If necessary, can you get a waiver of the application fee?
4. Is there a center or advisor on campus for undocumented students, and if so, what is the contact information?

Step 3: Become DACAmented

Deferred Action for Childhood Arrivals (DACA) status allows you to gain a social security number and eligibility for legal work within the United States. If you have not already applied, do so as soon as possible. As of this writing, fees are $465 and the form cannot be electronically submitted. Go to uscis.gov to find out more.

You may request DACA if you:

- Were under the age of 31 as of June 15, 2012.
- Came to the United States before reaching your 16th birthday.
- Have continuously resided in the United States since June 15, 2007, up to the present time.

- Were physically present in the United States on June 15, 2012, and at the time of making your request for consideration of deferred action with USCIS.
- Had no lawful status on June 15, 2012.
- Are currently in school, have graduated or obtained a certificate of completion from high school, have obtained a general education development (GED) certificate, or are an honorably discharged veteran of the Coast Guard or Armed Forces of the United States.
- Have not been convicted of a felony, significant misdemeanor, or three or more other misdemeanors, and do not otherwise pose a threat to national security or public safety.

Once you are DACAamented you can get a Social Security number, get a job, connect with other students, and become part of a larger community. You may complete and submit the FAFSA (though you still will not be eligible for federal financial aid), but you are not required to. Some colleges may request it; the requirements are different from institution to institution.

One important note: If you are a man you will absolutely need to register with the Selective Service System ("the draft") when you turn 18. If you have already received DACA status and have an SSN, you can do so online. If you don't yet have an SSN, you can file on paper; the sss.gov website has all the specifics. You do not need to be concerned that the Selective Service System is going to report you to immigration authorities. The website says:

> The Selective Service System has not now, or in the past, collected or shared any information which would indicate a man's immigration status, either documented or undocumented. Selective Service has no authority to collect such information, has no use for it, and it is irrelevant to the registration requirement. Consequently, there is no immigration data to share with anyone.

Step 4: Apply, consider your offers, and do the math

As you complete your applications, we recommend that you do not feel embarrassed about your undocumented status, but instead, embrace it; make it a part of your story, personal statement, or essay, if you can, and remind colleges of what an ambitious student you have been in the face of this particular adversity. And just as with a documented student, you will need to submit your applications, consider any offers that appear in May, and *do the math* about what you can afford. You do not need a Social Security Number to enroll, so if your DACA status is delayed or you are ineligible for any reason, do not worry about starting college in the fall.

Other resources

Many colleges and university systems make their undocumented students a priority. For example, the University of California system, Loyola University Chicago, and the University of Washington all have web pages that are helpful and supportive. As you collect college names and stats for your MAP, be sure to Google the "name of the school + undocumented students." Additionally, both the U.S. Department of Education (studentaid.ed.gov) and the National Association of Student Financial Aid Administrators (nasfaa.org) have fact sheets for undocumented students that you can download.

You are also eligible for private scholarships aimed at the DREAM community, such as thedream.us, the Becas Univision Scholarship, and the Ascend Educational Fund, to name a few. Check websites to find out more, but our general advice is that you should be judicious about how much of your time is spent applying for private scholarships.

Other than the specifics listed in this chapter, the rest of this book still applies to you and your family—so get reading, and good luck!

For Homeless and/or Unaccompanied Students

You MAY CURRENTLY be homeless, but despite how it may feel, you are not helpless, invisible, or alone. The number of homeless children hit a record high in 2014, when more than 1.36 million homeless children were enrolled in public schools from kindergarten through 12th grade.[1] That's nearly 2.5 percent of the 55 million school-age children in the United States, or one out of every 50 children.[2] Of those 1.36 million, 88,966 of them were unaccompanied, or did not have a parent or guardian taking care of them.

You have not been forgotten. In 2001, the Federal Government passed the McKinney-Vento Homeless Assistance Act (Title X, Part C of the Elementary and Secondary Education Act). McKinney-Vento provides a clear and excellent path for you to access resources to go to college. In December 2015, President Obama signed into law the Every Student Succeeds Act (ESSA) with new provisions for the homeless.

Though you may perceive your lack of an address, parent or guardian, financial support, or even identification as insurmountable obstacles, we promise you that these issues are not going to hold you back from applying to and financing a college education. The following steps will help you to get on track.

Who is homeless and/or unaccompanied?

McKinney-Vento defines an unaccompanied child or youth (homeless children) as:

A. individuals who lack a fixed, regular, and adequate nighttime residence.

B. includes

1. children and youths who are sharing the housing of other persons due to loss of housing, economic hardship, or similar reason; are living in motels, hotels, trailer parks, or camping grounds due to the lack of alternative accommodations; are living in emergency or transitional shelters; are abandoned in hospitals; or are awaiting foster care placement.

2. children and youths who have a primary nighttime residence that is a public or private place not designed for or ordinarily used as a regular sleeping accommodation for human beings.

3. children and youths who are living in cars, parks, public spaces, abandoned buildings, substandard housing, bus or train stations, or similar settings.

4. migratory children who qualify as homeless for the purposes of this subtitle because the children are living in certain circumstances.

Step 1: Find your McKinney-Vento liaison

Broadly, every homeless and/or unaccompanied student comes from a different situation, and there is no single one-size-fits-all solution. That's why McKinney-Vento has placed a designated liaison in your school, a staff member who has been trained and understands the hurdles you face and the programs and services that are possible and is there just for you. Your McKinney-Vento liaison could be a counselor, a teacher, a coach, or any member of the school's faculty or staff, and that person is going to be your greatest resource and advocate in the college application process.

Step 2: Obtain your letter of determination

Your McKinney-Vento liaison will need to officially determine that you are eligible for McKinney-Vento services. Without this written letter of determination, you may need to prove or describe your situation again, and again, and again.

Your liaison will ask you a series of questions that are designed to assess your living situation without violating your privacy or the protections you and your family have under federal law. Questions to determine your eligibility will consist of the following:

- Is this a permanent arrangement or just temporary?
- Are you looking for another place to live?
- Do you plan to move out soon?
- Why are you staying in your current place?
- Where were you living right before this place? Why did you leave?
- Where would you go if you couldn't stay where you are?
- Are you staying with friends/relatives just for a little while?
- Did you and your friends/relatives decide to move in together and share a home and expenses for the long term? Or is this a temporary situation for you?
- Could your friends/relatives ask you to leave if they wanted to?
- Are you all sharing the home equally, or are you more like guests in the home?
- Do you stay in the same place every night?
- Do you have a key to the place where you are living?
- Do you move around a lot?
- How long have you been at that place? How long do you plan to stay?
- How long did you live in your last place?

- How many people are living in the home? How many bedrooms/bathrooms does it have?
- Are you and your children sharing a room? How many people are staying in one room?
- Are you and your children sleeping in a bedroom, or in a public area, like a dining room?
- Does the home have heat/electricity/running water?
- What condition is the home in?
- Does it keep out rain and wind?
- Is it safe?
- Is it warm and dry?

Your liaison is asking you these questions in order to help you become protected and funded by the McKinney-Vento Act. Your family, friends, and acquaintances will not be affected by your eligibility for these services; no one will get into trouble if you answer these questions honestly, though your first conversation with the liaison may feel scary and intrusive. We promise that your liaison is on your side. Their first priority is to ensure that you become safe, housed, fed, and remain in school.

Step 3: Begin the college search!

You will need to perform the same search we recommend for every other type of student using our MAP profile in Chapter 6. When calculating your cost of attendance, feel free to assume that your EFC will be zero. Rely on your liaison for help, and know that every college and university you are interested in should have a single point of contact for you. Please feel free to inquire with that contact as often as you want or need to; don't be shy. It is that person's job to communicate with you and make you aware of the college's policies and protocols for McKinney-Vento eligible students. If possible, reach out to another friend or adult who you trust to help you complete the MAP; it will take an afternoon or two of their time, and it's always helpful to discuss your dreams, goals, and priorities with people who know and care about you.

Step 4: Apply for admission and complete the FAFSA

You will need to complete and submit your college applications and FAFSA on time, like every other student. See Chapters 8 and 9 for more information. Rely on your liaison for help getting everything out on time and to provide you with a fixed address for use on the FAFSA. Your liaison may need to submit your Letter of Determination directly to each college after you file your FAFSA.

Step 5:Do an apples-to-apples comparison below the 8K Debt Challenge

For students in your situation, we are very concerned about the potential impact of debt. We strongly recommend that you do not exceed our $8K Debt Challenge, or take out more than a total of $32,000 in loans for all four years. Please read Chapter 3 carefully.

Additional resources

NCHE

The National Center for Homeless Education, an excellent, reliable, and respected resource, is funded by the federal Department of Education and can be found at nche.ed.gov, and provides services in both Spanish and English. The helpline is (800) 308-2145.

NAEHCY

The National Association for the Education of Homeless Children and Youth is a not-for-profit organization that provides a broad range of community-based services, including local McKinney-Vento liaisons, educators, school counselors, social workers, registrars, nurses, child advocates, shelter staff, state and federal policy specialists, and partners from community-based and national non-profit organizations. Visit the website at naehcy.org, or text NAEHCY to 553377.

NOTES

Chapter 1

1. Troy Onink, "Federal Reserve: College Education Worth $830,000 More Than High School Diploma," *Forbes*, May 5, 2014.
2. Paul Krugman, "Graduates Versus Oligarchs," *The New York Times*, February 27, 2006.
3. "Trends in College Pricing 2015," The College Board, thecollege board.org.
4. Mark Krantrowitz, "Ask Kanthro," Fastweb.com, September 22, 2009.
5. *Digest of Education Statistics*, NCES, Table 326.10, nces.ed.goc, 2014.
6. Anya Kamanetz, "Clinton's Free-Tuition Promise: What Would It Cost? How Would It Work?," *All Things Considered*, National Public Radio, July 28, 2016.

Chapter 2

1. Alexander W. Astin, *What Matters in College: Four Critical Years Revisited*, Jossey-Bass Inc, San Francisco: 1993, 338.

Chapter 3

1. "Contexts of Postsecondary Education," U.S. Department of Education, nces.ed.gov.

Chapter 6

1. National Center for Education Statistics, U.S. Department of Education, nces.gov.
2. COAs mentioned here come from the colleges' own websites. Acceptance and enrollment data comes from the College Board, collegeboard.com.

Chapter 15

1. U.S. Department of Education, ED Data Express, eddataexpress.gov, 2013–14.
2. National Center for Education Statistics, Fast Facts 2016, nces .ed.gov.

INDEX

253